The Book of Psalms

Toni Craven

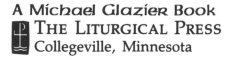

A Michael Glazier Book
THE LITURGICAL PRESS
Collegeville, Minnesota

DEDICATION

For Ann Richards

———

MESSAGE OF BIBLICAL SPIRITUALITY
Editorial Director: Carolyn Osiek, R.S.C.J.

Volume 6

A Michael Glazier Book published by The Liturgical Press

1   2   3   4   5   6   7   8   9

Library of Congress Cataloging-in-Publication Data

Craven, Toni.
    The book of Psalms / Toni Craven.
        p.   cm. — (Message of biblical spirituality ; v. 6)
    Includes bibliographical references.
    ISBN 0-8146-5556-4. — ISBN 0-8146-5572-6 (pbk.)
    1. Bible. O.T. Psalms—Devotional use. 2. Prayer—Biblical teaching. 3. God—Biblical teaching.   I. Title. II. Series.
BS1430.2.C73 1992
223'.206—dc20   92-6239
                                          CIP

Contents

Editor's Preface

One of the characteristics of church life today is a revived interest in spirituality. There is a growing list of resources in this area, yet the need for more is not exhausted. People are yearning for guidance in living an integrated life of faith in which belief, attitude, affections, prayer, and action form a cohesive unity which gives meaning to their lives.

The biblical tradition is a rich resource for the variety of ways in which people have heard God's call to live a life of faith and fidelity. In each of the biblical books we have a witness to the initiative of God in human history and to the attempts of people not so different from ourselves to respond to the revelation of God's love and care.

The fifteen volumes in the *Message of Biblical Spirituality* series aim to provide ready access to the treasury of biblical faith. Modern social science has made us aware of how the particular way in which one views reality conditions the ways in which one will interpret experience and life itself. Each volume in this series is an attempt to retell and interpret the biblical story from within the faith perspective that originally formed it. Each seeks to portray what it is like to see God, the world, and oneself from a particular point of view and to search for ways to respond faithfully to that vision. We who are citizens of our twentieth century world cannot be people of the ancient biblical world, but we can grow closer to their experience and their faith and thus closer to God, through the living Word of God which is the Bible.

The series includes an international group of authors representing England, Ireland, Canada, and the United States, but whose life experience has included first-hand knowledge of many other countries. All are proven scholars and committed believers whose faith is as important to them as their scholarship. Each acts as interpreter of one part of the biblical tradition in order to enable its spiritual vitality to be passed on to others. It is our hope that through their labor the reader will be able to enter more deeply into the life of faith, hope, and love through a fuller understanding of an appreciation for the biblical Word as handed down to us by God's faithful witnesses, the biblical authors themselves.

Carolyn Osiek, R.S.C.J.
Associate Professor of New Testament Studies
Catholic Theological Union, Chicago

Introduction

This is a book about some of the beliefs, attitudes, and practices of prayer suggested in the Book of Psalms. It is written as a companion to Carroll Stuhlmueller's two volume commentary on the psalms in the Michael Glazier Old Testament Message series. Stuhlmueller's work presents analysis of each of the 150 psalms summarizing "the best of scholarship or that which seems the most enduring."[1] This book focuses on topics related to spirituality in the psalms and describes in general fashion some of the beliefs, attitudes, and practices implied in the psalms about those who prayed them and their understanding of the God to whom they prayed. Since analysis of individual psalms and generalizations about the spirituality of these prayers belong together, Stuhlmueller's book and others like those he recommends in his bibliography[2] helpfully accompany and enrich reading of this book.

The Book of Psalms is like a self-contained religious library of prayer in that it incorporates an enormously wide spectrum of issues and reflects various historical backgrounds. It includes many understandings of God and multiple expressions of what it means to be faithful to the covenant.[3] There are numerous be-

---

[1] Carroll Stuhlmueller, *Psalms 1*, Old Testament Message 21 (Wilmington, DE: Michael Glazier, Inc., 1983) 13.

[2] Stuhlmueller, *Psalms 2*, Old Testament Message 22, 223–226.

[3] William Bellinger, *Psalms: Reading and Studying the Book of Praises* (Peabody,

liefs, attitudes, and practices of prayer suggested in the Book of Psalms that express different "spiritualities." This book is a selective sampling of issues that seem dominant in the psalms or that suggest themselves to me as particularly helpful to understanding the spirituality of the Book of Psalms and the practice of prayer.

You should be aware that my perspective has shaped the issues selected for review in this book. As a feminist who cares deeply about God and God's people, two questions are almost always before me: Who is God? What does it mean to be faithful, individually and communally? I am convinced that examination of how we pray individually and communally—what we say and how we say it—tells a story of who we are and who God is for us. What we say to and about God quite literally creates and maintains our reality, either consciously or unconsciously.

Life is enhanced or inhibited by the personal and communal mythology that guides what we say to and about God. Our prayers tell a story of the inner drama whose plot we enact in our daily lives. I believe that conscious appreciation of the psalms as a rich storehouse of guiding ideas about who God is and what it means to be faithful can be a powerful tool for increased awareness and transformation.

Close reading and study of the psalms has greatly enhanced and expanded my appreciation of them as a rich inheritance of faith and a key to fuller understanding of God, self, and the believing community. Doorways to new perceptions about God, self, and community have sometimes opened where I did not suspect doorways even existed. Surprisingly, study has sometimes itself been an act of prayer, an experience of encounter with God. Marjorie J. Thompson describes a similar experiential convergence of meditative reading and prayer:

> Many of us have learned to think of prayer and the reading of scripture as wholly distinct from one another. . . . But what of meditative reflection with scripture—that unhurried dwelling with God's word that Benedictine tradition sometimes has

MA: Hendrickson Publisher, Inc., 1990) 2, adds "The book also forms a kind of summary of Old Testament theology, reflecting representative themes in the story of God and ancient Israel." See also G. W. Anderson, "Israel's Creed: Sung not Signed," *Scottish Journal of Theology* 16 (1963) 277–285.

likened to a cow chewing its cud? Here the image is one of gradually extracting full nourishment from a source of food. Many of us, perhaps, have experienced meditative reflection with scripture leading *to* prayer; what may strike us as novel is the notion that it can be engaged in *as prayer*.[4]

From the writing of this book, I have come to know that prayer and study are not necessarily mutually exclusive, though, of course, they can be. One can easily be separated from the other. But one can lead to the other, and one can be concurrent with the other. It is quite possible to cross the thresholds of study and prayer simultaneously. A reader who chooses can come to this same experiential discovery that studying the psalms can be an act of prayer.

The boundary between personal use of the psalms and other uses of them is also flexible. In worship settings, we are accustomed to hearing the words of the psalms spoken as if they were composed for our own liturgical use. We regularly sing portions of the psalms in hymns or recite bits of them in prayers. Individually and communally, we know the powerful experience of having these ancient words express our own beliefs and attitudes as if they were written just for us. The words of some psalms are timeless expressions that seem able to take on fresh, new meanings. There are times when it means something experientially "new" and personal to pray or to study venerable words like "the LORD is my shepherd, I shall not want" (Ps 23:1). In personal prayer, liturgical recitation, and study, the psalms can be intimate, immediate expressions of piety. The psalms are unquestionably a rich legacy from which we can learn a great deal about prayer, God's identity, and our own identity in relationship with God.

In a most perceptive article on "Spirituality in the Psalms," James L. Kugel traces the kinds of use of the psalms that resulted in their history of "reinterpretation" for new conditions. He suggests that some of the fundamental concepts in the psalms "might have begun to be 'spiritualized'—that is, decontextualized—from a very early time."[5] It seems that "as the Psalms became Scrip-

---

[4] Marjorie J. Thompson, "Praying *with* Scripture," *Weavings* (May/June 1990) 36.
[5] See Kugel's article in *Jewish Spirituality from the Bible through the Middle Ages*, World Spirituality: An Encyclopedic History of the Religious Quest 13, ed. Arthur Green (New York: Crossroad, 1988) 135.

ture, they did so with an interpretive strategy attached: they were not to be interpreted as a self-standing book of prayers or praises, any more than Proverbs was to be a self-standing collection of wise sayings."[6] The psalms are adjuncts to other experiences and other bodies of literature. The basic "spirituality" of the psalms is that they are not an end in themselves.

The psalms are not 150 models of the most correct or most perfect ways to pray. Their "rightness" about prayer is not in their individuality, but rather in a pattern their totality suggests. As a whole, the psalms legitimate multiple modalities of conversation with God, and model the "rightness" of every voice that speaks in faith to God. It is not surprising, then, that the psalms continually give rise to new beliefs, attitudes, and practices. Because of the "interpretive strategy" attached to the psalms, the fixity of their canonical number is not a restriction. The psalms validate multiple interpretations within the canonical collection itself as well as multiple reinterpretations born of use in new contexts. Ultimately, the psalms support the finding of one's own voice with God.

Roland Murphy is doubtlessly correct that the psalms "present most vividly the perennial dialogue between God and human beings."[7] The psalms as we now read, study, and pray them record only one-half of the conversation. Most often they express the sentiments of members of the community in dialogue with God. In only a very few prayers does God speak (see, for example, the prophetic prayers which incorporate God's voice, such as Pss 50, 75, 81, 95). On account of the dominance of human speech to God in the psalms, Athanasius, Bishop of Alexandria from 328 C.E., is reported to have said that while most of the Bible speaks *to* us, the Psalms speak *for us*.[8]

In their final canonical form, these conversations with God refuse systematic categorization. Study of the psalms discloses no regularized understanding of right words to pray, right ways to describe God, or even right practice of faithfulness. The psalms are prayers from the "heart" in its genuinely Hebraic sense as the seat of the whole person, including body, intellect, feeling,

---

[6] Ibid., 136.

[7] Roland E. Murphy, *The Psalms, Job*, Proclamation Commentaries, ed. Foster R. McCurley (Philadelphia: Fortress Press, 1977) 11.

[8] See Bernhard W. Anderson, *Out of the Depths: The Psalms Speak for Us Today*, Revised and Expanded Edition (Philadelphia: Westminster Press, 1983) 9.

intuition, imagination, will, and action. The psalms express and validate many ideas about God and faithfulness. The conviction that the covenant is real, meaningful, and worth conversing about with God undergirds a wide range of human expressions including complaint, praise, and thanksgiving.

Individual and communal expressions of belief, hope, and trust in the covenant animate the prayers. The essential belief kept in place by these prayers is that the God of the covenant is one who is with the people. The radical hope of the psalms is that God sees those things which enslave people, individually and communally, and wills deliverance. The mysterious trust that pervades these prayers is the disposition that God holds out a future of hope. Various life experiences reveal who God is and who the individuals and community are called to be. Maintenance of dynamic relationship with God, not the saying of a particular set of "right" words to or about God, matters most in the psalms.

The psalmists voice their individual and corporate fears, hopes, and desires to God because they are members of a covenant community. Life is structured and maintained by active participation in the dynamic process of upholding and shaping traditions about God, self, and community, which are consonant with inherited values yet at the same time open to modification. Other than the undeniable reality of God's existence, there is no description of God, self, or community in the Book of Psalms about which there is unanimous agreement.

Covenant is a dynamic, ever unfolding experiential ground of conversation with God in the psalms. The psalms model a variety of appropriate ways to relate to God; they do not prescribe the right words to say to God. They contain no one consistent portrayal of who God is, neither do they offer one definitive description of what it means to be a faithful individual or community. Instead, in an array of ways the psalms testify that life experiences—whatever they may be—are moments of revelation. Life experiences give rise to a variety of prayers as the psalmists choose directions and move towards increasing covenantal congruence with God.

It is the psalmists' way to decision, movement, and choice of direction that this book seeks to explore. The topics examined cluster around three major headings:

I. THOSE WHO PRAYED THE PSALMS

II. THE GOD OF THE PSALMISTS

III. PRAYER AS A VEHICLE FOR UNDERSTANDING GOD AND SELF

Part I includes discussion of the types of prayers found in the Psalter; the language of prayer; anger and praise; and happiness and prayer. Part II surveys selected traditions and conventions of faith in the psalms; conceptions and names of God; poetic characterizations of God; and understandings of God's justice. Part III looks at wholeheartedness in prayer; the way of an individual and a community before God; and what this study of the psalms suggests about beliefs, attitudes, and practices of prayer.

The orientation of this study is the same as that already stated by Stuhlmueller: "We seek most of all to put this scholarship to the service of one's faith in a personal God, one's fuller participation in church life and worship, one's outreach in devotional piety and daily contemplation."[9] The goal of his commentary is "to enable the reader to pray the psalms ever more devoutly, to hear the voice of God ever more distinctly with each syllable."[10] This book shares that same goal by enlarging understanding of the beliefs, attitudes, and practices of prayer indicated in the psalms and the reader's own religious life as well. With Stuhlmueller, I believe, "Our own prayer today, to be authentic, must absorb the spirit of our ancestors in the faith."[11] I also believe that the spirit of our ancestors of faith is one found not in reductionist statements about the psalms, but rather by recognition of the plurality of beliefs, attitudes, and practices of prayer contained in the Book of Psalms. It is not a question of one way of prayer being better than the other, but rather a fundamental attitude of inclusivity in which both one way and another emerge as appropriate. We will see that the psalms teach an enlarged acceptance of ways of response to God that legitimate faithfulness as "both this and that."

[9] Stuhlmueller, *Psalms 1*, 13.
[10] Ibid., 11.
[11] Ibid.

A Prayer for Proceeding

O God, Source of all life, grant us the courage to come before you both when our hearts are broken and when our hearts are joyful. Make your living presence real to us that we might know you better and so learn to know ourselves more fully in the light of your transforming power.

Give us senses alert to your stirring in our hearts. Be with us as we choose directions and take steps to accomplish the tasks which are ours to do. Holy Mystery, allow us to move more purposefully toward the divine-human congruence to which we are called.

In confidence, we pray:

O YHWH, our God,
how majestic is your name in all the earth!
Your glory is chanted above the heavens.
You have founded a bulwark to still the enemy and all foes.
When we look at your heavens, the work of your fingers,
the moon and the stars which you have established;
Who are we that you are mindful of us,
mere human beings that you do care for us?
You have made us little less than yourself,
and you crown us with glory and honor.
You have given us dominion over the works of your hands;
You have put all things under our feet.
You, O God, transform our inmost desires
and give us the courage to be who you have called us to be.
You set straight our selfishness, illusions, fears, and unbelief.
You summon us to new wholeness and congruence.
You, O God, renew our belief, hope, and trust
that you are with us, that you see those things which
bind us, that you will to deliver us, and that you hold
out to us a future whose features are as yet undisclosed.
O YHWH, our God,
how majestic is your name in all the earth!

I. THOSE WHO PRAYED THE PSALMS

We trust in you at all times
and pour out our hearts before you;
for you are our refuge.
Ps 62:8[1]

1

Types of Prayer

CANONICAL SHAPE AND TITLE

In the Hebrew Bible the present title of the entire collection of the psalms is *tehillim*, which means "praises." In the Septuagint (Greek version) the prevailing title is *psalmoi*, suggesting songs sung to the accompaniment of stringed instruments. The English Bible title *Psalms* is taken from the Septuagint and the New Testament (see Luke 20:42; 24:44; Acts 1:20; 13:33, 35).

The Book of Psalms is a collection of 150 prayers that are divided into five books. Each book concludes with a doxology, a prayer of praise to God. Book I contains Psalms 1–41, with a concluding doxology in Ps 41:13. Book II contains Psalms 42–72, with a concluding doxology in Ps 72:18-19. Book III consists of Psalms 73–89, with a doxology in Ps 89:52. Book IV contains Psalms 90–106, with a concluding doxology in Ps 106:48. And Book V contains Psalms 107–150, with Psalm 150 the final doxology for the whole Psalter.

---

[1] Translation from *The New Companion to the Breviary with Seasonal Supplement* (Indianapolis, IN: Psalter, 1988) 45. The Carmelites of Indianapolis have adapted this translation for use in prayer from the Revised Standard Version of the Bible. See Eileen Schuller, "Inclusive-Language Psalters," *The Bible Today* 26:3 (May 1988) 173–79, for a helpful review of other currently available inclusive-language translations of the psalms.

This five-fold structure of the Psalter may be patterned after the Pentateuch (Torah), which contains five books (Genesis, Exodus, Leviticus, Numbers, Deuteronomy), though the reason for the five divisions is nowhere stated in the Book of Psalms itself and is no longer clear to modern interpreters. In its present form, the Book of Psalms is a collection of religious poems that are sometimes spoken of as "the hymnbook of the Second Temple."[2] The Book of Psalms was given its final shape for usage in the second temple of Zerubbabel, rebuilt in 520–515 B.C.E.[3] Perhaps the five divisions of the book suited the liturgical calendar of this sixth century second temple, though as Murphy points out, "we are quite ignorant of the liturgy of the second temple."[4]

We are equally ignorant about the date of composition for most of the psalms. It is probable that a good number of them were composed during the pre-exilic time of David and Solomon (tenth century B.C.E.), and that some are even earlier.[5] But as with reasons for the five-fold arrangement and knowledge about their usage in the second temple, so with dating—very little is known about the historical details of the composition of the psalms.

It is likely that the prayers contained in the Book of Psalms include rearrangements and elaboration of prayers that circulated prior to their usage by the post-exilic community. Points of contact between the psalms themselves and with other portions of Scripture make it clear that certain prayers were re-used and reinterpreted in the process of their collection. For instance, Psalm 14 is repeated as Psalm 53. Psalm 18 is found in a slightly different form in 2 Samuel 22. Seemingly related pieces of understandings of the ark appear in passages like Ps 105:4 = 1 Chr 16:11;

---

[2] Stuhlmueller's "Introduction" to *Psalms 1,* 15–55, presents a very helpful discussion of the canonical shape of the Book of Psalms, texts and versions, Hebrew poetry, and literary forms. Like Stuhlmueller, I will refer to individual psalms according to the enumeration and versification of the Revised Standard Version.

[3] B.C.E. is an abbreviation for Before the Common Era. C.E. refers to Common Era. These abbreviations have replaced the older dating conventions of B.C. (Before Christ) and A.D. (Year of Our Lord) in recent times in an effort at inclusive dating.

[4] Murphy, *The Psalms, Job,* 35.

[5] See Arthur Weiser, *The Psalms,* Old Testament Library, trans. Herbert Hartwell (Philadelphia: Westminster Press, 1962) 95–101, for information about the collection of the psalms. For a reconstruction of the historical process by which the Psalter took its present shape, see Walter Harrelson, *Interpreting the Old Testament* (New York: Holt, Rinehart and Winston, Inc., 1964) 407–408.

Ps 96:6 = 1 Chr 16:27, even though Psalm 132 is the only psalm which explicitly refers to the ark (v. 8).

Commonalities between the psalms and other Mesopotamian, Canaanite, and Egyptian prayers are well-established. We have found no "psalter" among any of Israel's neighbors, but striking resemblance of phrases and even whole poetic lines have been documented.[6] For example, in "Prayer of Lamentation to Ishtar" (the Babylonian Queen of Heaven and most potent God of fertility, war, and love), we read:

> How long, O my Lady, shall my adversaries be looking
> upon me,
> In lying and untruth shall they plan evil against me,
> Shall my pursuers and those who exult over me rage
> against me?
> How long, O my Lady, shall the crippled and weak seek
> me out? . . .
> Let my prayers and my supplications come to thee.
> Let thy great mercy be upon me.[7]

In another Babylonian parallel, a lament of Nebuchadnezzar I, we read:

> Yet how long with me,
> Yet how long in my land,
> Yet how long in my people?
> Until when, Lord of Babylon,
> This groaning and depression?
> This weeping and grieving?
> This lamenting and weeping?
> Do you tarry in the camp of the enemy?[8]

---

[6] Mitchell Dahood's influential three volume Anchor Bible commentary on the Psalms and over one hundred articles on this topic have taught us much about the strengths and weaknesses of comparative studies. For introduction to these issues and bibliographic suggestions, see Peter C. Craigie, *Psalms 1–50*, Word Biblical Commentary 19, ed. John D. W. Watts (Waco, TX: Word Books, Publisher, 1983) 48–56.

[7] "Prayer of Lamentation to Ishtar," trans. F. J. Stephens, *Ancient Near Eastern Texts*, ed. J. B. Pritchard (2d ed.; Princeton: Princeton University, 1955) 384–385. See, Bellinger, *Psalms*, 4–7, for further elaboration.

[8] As quoted in Hans-Joakim Kraus, *Psalms 1–59*, trans. Hilton C. Oswald (Minneapolis, MN: Augsburg Publishing House, 1988) 214.

And in Psalm 13, comparable phrases and ideas appear, but now in address to YHWH, the God of Israel:

> How long, YHWH? Will you forget me for ever?
>   How long will you hide your face from me?
> How long must I bear pain in my soul,
>   and have sorrow in my heart all the day?
> How long shall my enemy be exalted over me?
> Consider and answer me, YHWH my God;
>   lighten my eyes, lest I sleep the sleep of death;
> lest my enemy say, "I have prevailed over him";[9]
>   lest my foes rejoice because I am shaken.

The psalms are now arranged as a collection of collections. All but thirty-four, the so called "orphan psalms," are titled with superscriptions. The titles include references to literary forms, musical annotations, and proper names associated either as patron or author of individual psalms.[10] The titles yield little historically reliable information, and some of them even seem incorrect. For instance Psalm 30, which is a private prayer of thanksgiving after an illness, is titled, "A Psalm of David, A Song at the Dedication of the Temple." The incongruity of the title with the content of the prayer suggests that the setting of the psalm changed radically at a later stage of usage. How such changes occurred, we simply do not understand. The titles, though impossible to comprehend fully, do seemingly represent later efforts by the community to classify the usage of the psalms during the process of their assemblage as a collection of collections.[11]

---

[9] Reading with the RSV and the Hebrew "over him." NRSV deletes the masculine reference reading "I have prevailed." I have made the decision to leave pronouns that indicate human gender intact in biblical references. When references in the psalms are to males, I will not edit the texts. I want to be clear that while I find it helpful for study to leave gender identifications intact in order to more fully appreciate the speaker's point of view, I never use male pronouns as inclusive when I reflect in general terms on the psalms. I presume that readers addressed in this book are both female and male and that the psalms are a heritage belonging to us all.

[10] For additional information about the superscriptions, see Stuhlmueller, *Psalms* 1, 22–27.

[11] The arrangement of the various collections is helpfully diagrammed in Claus Westermann's, *Handbook to the Old Testament* (Minneapolis, MN: Augsburg Publishing House, 1976) 215–216.

The titles designate seventy-three psalms "of David," meaning either "by" David or "for" David (Pss 3–9, 11–32, 34–41, 51–65, 68–70, 86, 101, 103, 108–110, 122, 124, 131, 133 [in the Hebrew Bible but not in English translations], 138–145). It is not clear that the psalm titles containing the name of David were intended to communicate authorship, though Davidic authorship is surely suggested by tradition and the note in Ps 72:20 that "the prayers of David son of Jesse are ended."[12] The psalms themselves recognize more than Davidic connections in those prayers attributed to Moses (Ps 90), Solomon (Pss 72, 127), Jeduthun (Pss 39, 62, 77), Heman (Ps 88), and Ethan (Ps 89). Eleven are attributed to the Korahites (Pss 42, 44–49, 84, 85, 87, 88), and twelve to Asaph (Pss 50, 73–83).

There are two major liturgical collections in Books IV and V. The Songs of Ascent (Pss 120–134) provide devotional inspiration for those on pilgrimage to and from Jerusalem. The Hallel psalms (Pss 113–118) and those containing the ritual refrain Hallelujah, "Praise the Lord" in some translations, (Pss 105, 106, 111–112, 135, 146–150) likely took shape for temple ceremonies.

LITERARY FORMS

Another way to classify the psalms is to group them according to their genre or literary type.[13] The Book of Psalms, as we will

---

[12] In "Spirituality of the Psalms," Kugel discusses in great detail the significance of Davidic authorship both in tradition and in the gradual "Scripturalization" of the psalms, 113–144. He points out that the tradition that David wrote the psalms "continued to gain steam" with the passage of time. The Septuagint Psalter, the Syriac apocryphal psalms, and the Peshitta contain more Davidic attributions than the Masoretic Text (135). "David continued to loom before the readers of Scripture as the man of prayer *par excellence*, the human sinner who could return as a penitent and seek forgiveness, or in time of distress 'pour forth my complaint' (Ps 142:2)," 136.

[13] Hermann Gunkel (1862–1932) is responsible for the "form-critical" approach to the study of the psalms which has become the most widely utilized approach in twentieth-century research. He wanted to understand the literary types of the psalms and their functional relationship to the history of the people *(Sitz im Leben)*. For details and an assessment of his work, see John H. Hayes, *An Introduction to Old Testament Study* (Nashville, TN: Abingdon, 1979) 287–317.

analyze it, contains nine types of prayers. *Hymns of Praise* celebrate God as the creator of the universe and the sustaining controller of history. *Enthronement Psalms* are marked by the cultic
exclamation "YHWH reigns" or "YHWH is king." The *Songs of
Zion* are psalms that focus on Jerusalem or Zion as the place of
God's presence. *Laments* are prayers of complaint about crisis situations involving personal enemies, sickness, military affairs, concern for the sanctuary, friends who no longer are friends,
problems with God's being inaccessible, or other distressing situations. *Prayers of Thanksgiving and Trust* praise God for deliverance already experienced. *Royal Psalms* express the concerns of
the king. *Liturgical Psalms* reflect either solo or choral parts used
in entrance liturgies, judgment liturgies, and liturgies of divine
protection. *Wisdom Psalms* are often characterized by advice concerning behavior, contrast between the wicked and the just, "better" or "happy" sayings, and inclusion of the "fear of the Lord"
formula. *Mixed Types* combine elements from various kinds of
psalms.

There is considerable difference of opinion among scholars
about the classification of the psalms according to literary type.[14]
There are too many uncertainties and too much overlapping between the categories to allow exact classification. Nonetheless,
for the purpose of having a sense of the distribution of types of
prayers contained in the Book of Psalms, I suggest the following
division of the 150 prayers.

PSALM TYPES

15 Hymns of Praise: 8, 19, 33, 65, 100, 104, 113, 114, 117, 145, 146,
   147, 148, 149, 150
7 Enthronement Psalms: 29, 47, 93, 96, 97, 98, 99
6 Songs of Zion: 46, 48, 76, 84, 87, 122
60 Laments:
   44 Individual: 3, 4, 5, 6, 7, 9–10, 13, 17, 22, 25, 26, 28, 31, 35,
      38, 39, 42–43, 51, 52, 54, 55, 56, 57, 59, 61, 63, 64, 69, 70, 71,
      77, 86, 88, 102, 109, 120, 130, 139, 140, 141, 142, 143
   16 Communal: 12, 14(=53), 44, 53(=14), 58, 60, 74, 79, 80, 83,
      85, 90, 123, 126, 129, 137

---

[14] Compare, for example, Stuhlmueller's outline, *Psalms 1*, 53–55.

17 Prayers of Thanksgiving and Trust: 11, 16, 23, 30, 62, 66, 67, 75, 92, 103, 107, 116, 118, 124, 125, 131, 138

9 Royal Psalms: 2, 18, 20, 21, 45, 72, 101, 110, 132

15 Liturgical Psalms:

  2 Entrance Liturgies: 15, 24

  4 Judgment Liturgies: 50, 81, 82, 95

  9 Liturgies of Divine Protection: 78, 91, 105, 106, 115, 121, 134, 135, 136

12 Wisdom Psalms: 1, 32, 34, 37, 49, 73, 111, 112, 119, 127, 128, 133

9 Mixed Types: 27, 36, 40, 41, 68, 89, 94, 108, 144

The psalms are poetic prayers or songs addressed by individuals or the community to God. The remainder of this chapter illustrates the variety of life experiences reflected in the psalms. As we shall see, all experiences of life—mountain tops, level-places, and deep valleys—are appropriate occasions for prayers of worship and praise.

SAMPLE TYPES

Hymns

Ten percent of the psalms are hymns or prayers of praise. These prayers typically celebrate God as creator and sustaining controller of history. They are ecstatic "mountain top" celebrations of wondrous faith in a reliable, trustworthy God. Often they follow a threefold A-B-A pattern of an opening call to worship (A), followed by the motive or reason for praise (B), with a concluding recapitulation of the opening (A). Imperatives are regularly employed to express the mood of certainty that God's creation and order for the world is sure and worthy of praise.

Psalm 117 is an example hymn in miniature. It opens with a comprehensive imperative summoning all to worship:

A Praise the LORD, all nations!

    Extol [God], all peoples! (v. 1)[15]

---

[15] The issue of how to best translate Hebrew masculine pronouns for God and human beings is one with which many modern translators are struggling. The 1985 English-language edition of the New Jerusalem Bible has made a serious effort to use inclusive terms when referring to the human family, but for the most part decided to leave masculine reference to God alone. In this book, I am going to replace all masculine pronouns for God with a bracketed substitute pronoun

Next, as is characteristic in hymns, the preposition "for" appears to introduce the motive element. Unquestionable confidence in God's steadfast faithfulness is the reason for praise:

> B   For great is [God's] steadfast love toward us;
>   and the faithfulness of the LORD endures for ever. (v. 2)

Finally, the hymn ends as it began, recapitulating:

> A   Praise the LORD! (v. 3).

In three short verses, this briefest of all psalms, expresses a sense of well-being. The psalmist is free from anxiety because God is good and worthy of praise from all. The world of this psalmist is protected by God's "sacred canopy."[16]

Psalm 8 follows this same hymnic pattern and reflects a similar sense of well-being, though the details are more fully developed. Identical expression of praise in verses 1 and 9 open and close the psalm:

> O LORD, our Lord,[17]
> how majestic is your name in all the earth!

or noun. I take as my model for these changes the ancient practice of the Jewish scribes known in Hebrew as "kethibh"/"qere" (pronounced "kuh-theev"/kuh-ray"), where what is "written" in the text is enunciated or "read" differently as noted in the margin of the Hebrew Bible. In Chapter 6 when we look at names for God in the psalms, we will take note of the regular practice in the Hebrew Bible of pronouncing the consonants YHWH (which NJB regularly translates, "Yahweh," as the text is "written") as the name "adonay" (Lord), a masculine title of honor. Fear of profaning the holiness of the name "Yahweh" led the scribes to see the written consonants YHWH but to substitute the spoken title "adonay." The practice of seeing one word and saying another is an ancient Masoretic practice, dating from the late post-exilic period. Out of reverence for the mystery of God's identity, I will adapt this ancient practice and substitute a bracketed expression for all gender specific reference to the Holy One in this book when the biblical texts specify gender for God. Out of respect for the Jewish preference to avoid pronouncing the name of God, whenever possible I will leave the tetragrammaton unvocalized in the text as YHWH.

[16] On the social function accomplished by psalms which praise the reliability of God's order for the community, see Walter Brueggemann, *The Message of the Psalms*, Augsburg Old Testament Studies (Minneapolis, MN: Augsburg Publishing House, 1984) 25–28.

[17] Notice the difference between LORD which reflects the Hebrew name YHWH and *Lord* which is adonay, lord or master, in Hebrew. As already noted, we will discuss the significance of these names in Chapter 6.

In the motive section of this prayer (vv. 1b-8), the identity of the speaker shifts from the communal voice addressing "our Lord" to that of an individual man looking at the night sky. The reason for this hymn is disclosed as reverence for the order of God's universe (v. 3) and enhanced appreciation of the wondrousness of being a human who is charged with governance of creation (vv. 4-8). Praise of God the creator reveals a new sense of human dignity to this psalmist:

> 1bYou whose glory above the heavens is chanted
> 2 by the mouth of babes and infants,
>> you have founded a bulwark because of your foes,
>> to still the enemy and the avenger.
> 3When I look at your heavens, the work of your fingers,
>> the moon and the stars which you have established;
> 4what is a human that you are mindful of him,
>> and a mortal that you do care for him?
> 5Yet you have made him little less than God,
>> and crown him with glory and honor.
> 6You have given him dominion over
>> the works of your hands;
>> you have put all things under his feet,
> 7all sheep and oxen,
>> and also the beasts of the field,
> 8the birds of the air, and the fish of the sea,
>> whatever passes along the paths of the sea.

Of particular interest are vv. 4-5 which highlight the psalmist's understanding that God created human beings with special dignity, "little less than God," and crowned humanity "with glory and honor." In this text we hear a male speaker who has looked at the wonder of the night sky shift his focus from outward consideration to personal reflection.

"Little less than God" (v. 5) likely originally read "little less than the gods," meaning the heavenly assembly. In the Septuagint, the Greek substitutes the word "angels." In either version, the point is that humanity's place in creation is an extraordinary gift from God. The Hebrew psalmist daringly claims that human beings are made by God, are like God, and are crowned by God with honor and glory. It is significant that this profound sense of God's care and intention for humanity is framed by exclamations praising God's majestic name (vv. 1, 9). This hymn celebrating God's name occasioned fuller appreciation of what it meant to be God's agent in the world by right of God's created order. Enhanced self-understanding is encircled by references to God's majestic name and authorized by God's order of creation.

Enthronement Psalms

Like hymns, the seven enthronement psalms are prayers of praise. The substance of the praise, however, is more specifically restricted to praise of God's reign as king.[18] The stylistic signal is not simply an A-B-A form but the inclusion of the formula "YHWH reigns" (Pss 93:1; 96:10; 97:1; 99:1) "God reigns" (Ps 47:8), or the expression that "YHWH is king" (Pss 29:10; 98:6). These prayers of praise are affirmations that God's governance extends to the whole universe.[19]

Songs of Zion

The six songs of Zion are also like the hymns of praise, though special content defines these prayers as a separate category. In Psalms 46, 48, 76, 84, 87, and 122, praise of Jerusalem or Zion is the main topic. The holy city of Jerusalem was the Jebusite city captured by David, the place where the temple was built, the center of God's presence among the people. These prayers praise the city of God as a place of special protection and refuge. Inspired by Psalm 46, "A Mighty Fortress Is Our God," Martin Luther's famous hymn, expresses the confident sentiment of this group of psalms. Jerusalem or Zion is a place of protected refuge.

Laments

Laments are prayers of complaint. Forty percent of the prayers of the Psalter are of this type. Numerically the dominant psalm type, laments reflect experiences in the depths of loneliness, frustration, and fearfulness. The attitude that YHWH is ready to hear the protestations of the dissatisfied is coupled with the practice

[18] For more on YHWH as King and Creator, see Stuhlmueller, *Psalms 2*, 77–78.
[19] For theological summary of the metaphor of God's kingship, see Brueggemann, *Message of the Psalms*, 150–152.

of unrestrained complaint. The psalmists are confident that if God willed to intervene, distress would be alleviated.

The conviction in these prayers is that the world of the individual or the community is out of order. In many cases, the disequilibrium is charged to God who has failed the psalmists or to enemies who are triumphing unfairly. Usually the psalmist claims innocence. Though we regularly pray the moving confession of Psalm 51 in our liturgies, the sentiment that on account of personal sin the psalmist stands in need of "a clean heart" or "a new and right spirit" (v. 10) is rare in the psalms.[20]

Laments are characterized by a six-fold structure:

1. Address to God
2. Complaint
3. Confession of Trust
4. Petition
5. Words of Assurance
6. Vow of Praise

The psalmists unrestrainedly complain to God about whatever personal or communal crisis occasions their prayer. One of the remarkable things about a lament is that despite the fact that God is frequently held responsible for the distress, the psalmists usually express unqualified trust in God's good intention for them.[21] Completely surrendering the situation to God, they freely petition God for whatever they desire. In Chapter 3, we will look more closely at some of the problems raised by expressions of anger and vindictiveness in some of the laments.

From narratives, we know that laments could include words of assurance spoken by a religious official. For example, after Hannah's lament (1 Samuel 1:10f.), Eli the priest spoke words of assurance that her prayer had been heard and that her petition for a child would be answered with the birth of a son, Samuel. In most of the laments in the Psalter it is difficult to distinguish words

---

[20] The ancient Church regarded Psalms 6, 32, 38, 51, 102, 130, and 143 as penitential psalms. However the theme of penitence is not particularly prominent in Psalms 6, 32, 102, or 143.

[21] Psalm 88 is unrelieved by hope in God's good intention for the psalmist. The psalmist cries out that God's wrath has swept over him like a torrent. Even so, the psalmist still directs his prayer to God, "day and night" (v. 1). Like Job, this psalmist looks to God for justice and deliverance.

of assurance because the speakers' parts are not identified (see Ps 12:5 for a likely example). It is possible that words of assurance were spoken but not recorded when a lament was prayed in a worship setting. A priest or another religious leader may have offered assurance in God's name that laments were rightly spoken and heard.

Vows of praise are promises to persevere in the covenant relationship by the doing of some act. Usually the vows in the lament psalms are modest promises to sing God's praises in the sanctuary or to offer a token of sacrifice.

Psalm 13 is a clear illustration of all the elements of a lament, except the word of assurance. The lament opens with an address to God and the two-fold complaint that God is absent and that the enemy is exalting:

> ¹How long, O LORD? Will you forget me for ever?
> How long will you hide your face from me?
> ²How long must I bear pain in my soul,
>   and have sorrow in my heart all the day?
> How long shall my enemy be exalted over me?

The petition of the psalmist expresses confidence that this pain can be alleviated if God listens:

> ³Consider and answer me, O LORD my God;
>   lighten my eyes, lest I sleep the sleep of death;
> ⁴lest my enemy say, "I have prevailed over him";
>   lest my foes rejoice because I am shaken.

By the conclusion of the psalm, despite experience of God's absence, the psalmist expresses trust:

> ⁵But I have trusted in your steadfast love.

The psalmist confidently concludes with a vow to persevere with joy:

> My heart will rejoice in your salvation.
> ⁶I will sing to the LORD,
>   because [God] has dealt bountifully with me.

In this prayer, honest complaint coupled with complete trust in God seems to effect relief for the psalmist. In misery the psalmist four times cries, "How long, O God?" (vv. 1-2). Yet the psalm ends with an expression of confident trust in God's steadfast love and expected joy in God's bountiful deliverance (vv. 5-6). The alteration of mood at the conclusion stands as a reminder that lament changed things for this worshiper.

Laments bespeak the knowledge that the individual or the community is not in control, that God is an agent of powerful change. Laments call God to act to bring order out of chaos, to restore the peace and wholeness of *shalom*. Spoken by those whose world is out of order to a God whose covenant offers the hope of renewed order, laments are powerful testimonies to the faith of a people who believed it appropriate to praise God from the depths of human distress with honest words of complaint.

Prayers of Thanksgiving and Trust

Nearly thirteen percent of the psalms are prayers of thanksgiving and trust. Many of these prayers are words spoken on the other side of a lament. God is praised as the one who delivered the individual or community from distress. Examples include expressions of confidence and gratitude like the following: "Though I walk through the valley of the shadow of death, I fear no evil; for you are with me; your rod and your staff, they comfort me" (Ps 23:4). Or "I will extol you, O LORD, for you have drawn me up, and have not let my foes rejoice over me. Oh LORD my God, I cried to you for help, and you have healed me" (Ps 30:1-2). In psalms of this type, the occasion and experience of deliverance are remembered by telling the inspiring story of how God transformed distress into gladness.

Psalm 116 is a classic example of a prayer of thanks and trust in which the psalmist testifies before the assembly how he loves God who rescued him in his time of distress. Psalm 116 inspires hope:

> I suffered distress and anguish.
> ⁴Then I called on the name of the LORD:
> "O LORD, I beseech you, save my life!"
> ⁵Gracious is the LORD, and righteous;
> our God is merciful.
> ⁶The LORD preserves the simple;
> when I was brought low, [God] saved me.

Royal Psalms

The nine royal psalms are the prayers for or by an earthly ruler. The content of these prayers is widely varied. Psalm 2 is a coronation prayer that contains the words of the newly enthroned king as well as God's own promise to him of universal rule. Psalm 18 is the thanksgiving prayer of a king who was triumphant in a battle. Psalm 20, probably composed to accompany a sacrifice before a battle, is a prayer said by an unnamed voice for the king. Paired with its preceding psalm, Psalm 21 is a prayer of thanksgiving that God answered the king's prayer. Psalm 45 is a royal wedding song sung to praise a king and a queen by a professional whose "tongue is like the pen of a ready scribe" (v. 1). Psalm 72 is a prayer of intercession for the king that he might be a righteous ruler. Psalm 101 is the personal prayer of one who wishes to use his juridical power rightly. Psalm 110, a prayer addressed to the king, includes two oracular statements from God (vv. 1, 4), each followed by statements of encouragement from an unnamed cultic official, (vv. 2-3; 5-7) perhaps a court prophet on the occasion of the installation of a new king or the anniversary of the coronation, that his kingship is authorized by God. Psalm 132, the last psalm in this group, is the prayer of an unnamed religious official said perhaps on the occasion of the anniversary of the temple's dedication, recalling how David brought the ark to Jerusalem and how God granted his dynasty privileges and power. In sum, royal psalms are prayers of or for earthly rulers.

Liturgical Psalms

This classification is difficult to define because in a broad sense most psalms in their final form might be listed here as having something to do with liturgical worship. This type of prayer, as included here, is meant to categorize fifteen psalms that seem to contain structured liturgical parts for either solo or choral recitation. The various voices in these prayers may once have reflected parts in liturgical rites carried out in the temple or some other religious center of the people.

Entrance Liturgies.   In a style suggestive of possible liturgical parts, Psalm 15 opens with an inquiry about who may be admitted to the temple and continues with the answer that those who come into God's presence should be blameless with regard to sins of the tongue and abuse of wealth. Psalm 24 asks who shall be allowed to stand in God's holy place, then answers that the one with clean hands and a pure heart will be allowed to enter the gates of the King of glory. These questions about fitness for worship and their answers seem to reflect different voices. Likely an individual or a group inquired of a priest or some other religious leader about right preparation for coming into God's presence.

Judgment Liturgies. God or a cultic official speaks a word of judgment to an assembly in psalms of this type. In Psalm 82, God judges the lesser gods in the heavenly council unjust and partial to the wicked. In Psalms 50, 81, and 95, God indicts the people assembled for worship.

> Hear, O my people, and I will speak, O Israel,
> I will testify against you. I am God, your God (Ps 50:7).

Psalm 50 continues that the people have brought abundant, unnecessary sacrifices to God who desires instead thanksgiving, prayer, and right speech from the faithful.

Psalm 81 is a more complicated liturgy in which first the people sing to God (vv. 1-5), then God reminds them of past acts of protection (vv. 6-7) and admonishes them for turning to other gods (vv. 8-12). Next, God appeals for obedience (vv. 13-14), promising, "I would feed you with the finest of the wheat, and with honey from the rock I would satisfy you" (v. 16). Embedded in this psalm is the divine indictment:

> Hear, O my people, while I admonish you!
> O Israel, if you would but listen to me! (Ps 81:8).

Psalm 95 opens similarly with a song of the people (vv. 1-7a) and continues with an admonishment from God that the people hearken to God's voice (vv. 7b-11).

Liturgies of Divine Protection. Psalms 78, 105, 106, 135, 136 call forth God's protection by reciting the history of God's dealing with the people. These historical story-telling psalms emphasize that disobedience and ingratitude provoke God's punishment, not blessing.

Psalms 91 and 121 are meditations on God's protection of the faithful which both contain dialogic passages of assurance (see 91:14-16 and 121:2-8).

Psalm 115 is a communal confession in which the covenant people reject their fears and receive a new blessing. Psalm 134 is a very brief liturgy which exhorts the servants of the Lord who stand by night in the house of the Lord to lift up their hands and bless YHWH.

Wisdom Psalms

The twelve wisdom psalms all share the feature of offering advice for daily living. They emphasize the choice of the way of righteousness over the way of wickedness. Murphy helpfully summarizes the eight characteristics of wisdom psalms as including: "a) the contrast between the just and the wicked; b) advice concerning conduct; c) fear of the Lord; d) the presence of comparisons and admonitions; e) alphabetic (acrostic) sequence of verses; f) 'better' sayings; g) the address to a 'son'; h) the 'blessed' (*'ashre*) formula."[22]

Psalm 37 is a classic example of these characteristics. The point of the prayer is to affirm that God rewards the righteous and punishes the wicked. The faithful are advised to fret not (v. 1), trust YHWH and do good (v. 3), commit their way to God (v. 5), be still and wait patiently for the LORD (v. 7), refrain from anger (v. 8), depart from evil and do good (v. 27), and keep to God's way (v. 34). Each letter of the Hebrew alphabet begins two verses of this elaborate acrostic prayer of an older person who testifies, "I have been young, and now am old; yet I have not seen the righteous forsaken or his children begging bread" (v. 25). "Better is a little that the righteous has than the abundance of the many wicked" (v. 16). Psalm 37, like the other wisdom psalms, ritualizes God's redeeming power in daily life. Rewards and punishments will be fairly realized according to the disposition of the wisdom psalms.

Mixed Types

The nine psalms listed under this heading are combinations of the preceding types. For instance, Psalm 27 contains a prayer of trust (vv. 1-6) and a lament (vv. 7-14). Psalm 36 contains two distinct parts: a wisdom psalm (vv. 1-4), and a hymn of praise (vv.

---

[22] Murphy, *The Psalms, Job*, 21.

5-9) that closes with a petition (vv. 10-12). Psalm 40 seems to reflect two different life situations, one of gratitude for deliverance (vv. 1-10), the other of grave affliction (vv. 11-17). And so it is with Psalms 41, 68, 89, 94, 108, 144. Psalm 108 is of special interest because it combines material from two existing psalms:

> Ps 108:1-5 = Ps 57:7-11
> Ps 108:6-13 = Ps 60:5-12

SUMMARY WORD ABOUT TYPES OF PRAYER

What is said to God is not the most important aspect of Israel's prayers. The right content of prayer is never defined in a programmatic way. Hymns, laments, prayers of thanksgiving, even an ode for a royal wedding (Ps 45)—all are equally appropriate and honored by inclusion in the Book of Psalms. That there are more laments than any other type of prayer does not mean that the best way to pray is to complain. One type of prayer is not valued more than the other types. The variety of prayers in the Psalter simply illustrates that prayer arises from lived experience. An amazing variety of experiences serve as opportunities for dialogue with God. The community has collected these prayers without any clue of a judgment that one kind of prayer is better than another. This collection of collections is a book quite astonishingly called *tehillim,* ''praises.''

In the psalms, a variety of experiences are appropriate beginning points for prayer. Concern for maintenance of the relationship between God and worshiper gives rise to assorted types of prayers. The preponderance of laments testify to the fact that negative experiences do not nullify praise. Laments do not isolate or cut off the one who prays from praising God or from the community of believers. Negative or positive life experiences are equal and legitimate experiences of the covenant. The pain of doubt about God, self, or others does not render the covenant meaningless. The joy of the certain knowledge that God protects the world does not prove the power of the covenant. A basic attitude of the psalmists is that covenant was, is, and will be. Prayer arising from any and all experience maintains covenant.

Prayers of all types are said and remembered for the sake of the present and future worshipers: ''Let this be recorded for a generation to come, so that a people yet unborn may praise the

LORD'' (Ps 102:18). Trust between God and present worshipers, in continuity with the experiences of past generations and exercised for future generations, grounds human existence. Prayers in good times and bad times were part of the remembered rhythm of life and relationship with God. Praise is a very flexible category that excludes no expression of contact with the Holy.

Finally, the verse with which we began this chapter says it all:

> We trust in you at all times
> and pour out our hearts before you;
> for you are our refuge (Ps 62:8).

Poetry is the flowering of ordinary possibilities.
It is the fruit of ordinary and natural choices.
This is its innocence and dignity.

Thomas Merton[1]

2

The Language of Prayer

The Book of Psalms is unique in all the Bible as the only book which consists entirely of prayers. The psalms rightly merit designation as "The Prayer Book of the Bible." While prayers are embedded in varying places in the Bible, no other book of the Bible is in its entirety a poetic collection of prayers. For instance, victory songs celebrating the deliverance at the sea appear on the lips of Moses and Miriam in Exodus 15, a lament is prayed by Hannah at Shiloh in 1 Samuel 1, and Elijah beseeches God to let the Widow of Zarephath's son come back to life in 1 Kings 17, but these prayers are parts of larger wholes. The story of the exodus; the story of Hannah's desire for a child; and the story of how the widow shared the last of her food with Elijah and was rewarded with a jar of meal and a cruse of oil that did not fail, but then experienced the death of her son and so went to the prophet and said, "What have you against me, O man of God?" (1 Kgs 17:18), these stories surround the prayers they contain and narrate the life experiences that gave rise to them.

The psalms are poetic speech in which the psalmists express an enormous range of understandings of God, self, and community as they talk to God in language that employs dynamic, and often extravagant imagery. The psalms tell their story in-between

---

[1] Thomas Merton, "Message to Poets," *Raids on the Unspeakable* (New York: New Directions, 1964) 159.

35

the lines of their poetic utterances, so to speak. Some superscriptions suggest possible life-settings. A classic example is the association of the sentiment "Create in me a clean heart, O God, and put a new and right spirit within me" in Psalm 51 with David, as a fitting prayer for him after the prophet Nathan had confronted him about his relationship with Bathsheba, the wife of Uriah the Hittite. But this association, like that of most of the superscriptions, is virtually impossible to prove. In fact, it is relatively easy in the case of Psalm 51 to point to the last two verses (vv. 18-19) of the psalm as contradictory evidence pointing not to the time of David (1000–961 B.C.E.), but to the time before the second temple (520–515 B.C.E.), or the rebuilding of the walls of Jerusalem in the time of Nehemiah (445 B.C.E.). Nonetheless, there is an impulse at work in the same superscriptions to provide narrative detail for the psalms. And this impulse vividly reminds us that the psalms are poems. Their poetic lines attract more than one interpretation. Narratives of all sorts have a way of attaching themselves to the psalms precisely because these prayers are poems. The timelessness of the psalms is directly related to the poetic nature of their language.

When the psalmists pour out their life experiences to God, they do so in poetry, not prose. To comprehend these prayers, we must allow them all the excesses and possibilities of poetry. C. S. Lewis says it this way:

> Most emphatically the Psalms must be read as poems; as lyrics, with all the licences and all the formalities, the hyperboles, the emotional rather than logical connections, which are proper to lyric poetry. They must be read as poems if they are to be understood; no less than French must be read as French or English as English. Otherwise we shall miss what is in them and think we see what is not.[2]

Christoph Barth calls the Book of Psalms "a *school* of prayer."[3] The poems produced by this "school" teach that prayer and poetry belong together. Just as French is French and English is English, prayer is poetry. Both prayer and poetry require attentive

---

[2] C. S. Lewis, *Reflections on the Psalms* (New York: Harcourt Brace Jovanovich, 1958) 3.

[3] Christoph Barth, *Introduction to the Psalms*, trans. R. A. Wilson (Oxford: Basil Blackwell, 1966) 36.

care to patterning what is said, expressive freedom with language, and a disposition to let the ordinary disclose the extraordinary.

In my study I have a crystal hanging in a west window that catches the afternoon sun and causes rainbows to dance across the walls of the room. As I tried to find words to tell about how poetry works in the psalms, it struck me that the poetic patterns in the prayers of the Psalter can be likened to the rainbow patterns reflected through such a crystal. When a faceted crystal catches the light, different patterns sparkle into focus with slight movements. From one direction, one set of reflections are refracted through the facets. Turned slightly, another set of images flash into focus. Slight movement changes perspective, sometimes repeating, sometimes enhancing, and sometimes even altering what is seen. The psalmists had the habit of using words in a way like this to say something one way and then to enhance or alter what was said by repeating the same thing in a similar or an opposite way. Passion and intensity, not haste, mark the poetry of the Psalter. Prayer is a catching of sunlight in words that allows us to see in a new way.

Repetition, which is the hallmark of Hebrew poetry, is called parallelism.[4] Elements from one poetic line appear in parallel lines. There are basically three kinds of parallelism in Hebrew poetry: synonymous, antithetical, and constructive.[5] Only the first two types can be observed in English translations. The third type depends on the arrangement of Hebrew words in which balance is achieved synthetically by repetition of similar or identical grammatical constructions in parallel lines. In constructive parallelism grammatical forms, such as participles, nouns, verbs, or other Hebrew parts of speech, appear in repeated patterns. Because the repetition is in grammatical forms, not in the meaning of the words, it is only by accident that constructively parallel Hebrew terms appear so in English translation.[6]

---

[4] For more detail, consult James Kugel, *The Idea of Biblical Poetry* (New Haven, CT: Yale University Press, 1981) and Stephen Geller, *Parallelism in Early Biblical Poetry* (Chico, CA: Scholars Press, 1979).

[5] I am using Robert Lowth's categories of parallelism. For fuller treatment, see Toni Craven, *Artistry and Faith in the Book of Judith,* Society of Biblical Literature Dissertation Series 70 (Chico, CA: Scholars Press, 1983) 21–34.

[6] Lowth cites Ps 135:7 as an example of constructive or synthetic parallelism. His English translation shows the repetition of three participial forms (emphasis mine) with unrelated meanings:

Causing the vapours to descend from the ends of the earth;

Synonymous parallelism is repetition of similar or identical words or phrases. Consider the variety in the following illustrations of synonymous parallelism which show repetitions of words with corresponding meanings at the beginning of lines, at the end of lines, and at the end of one line and the beginning of the next:

> Hear a just cause, O Lord;
>> attend to my cry!
> Give ear to my prayer from lips free of deceit! (Ps 17:1).

> Fret not yourself because of the wicked,
>> be not envious of wrongdoers! (Ps 37:1).

> Unless the Lord builds the house,
>> those who build it labor in vain.
> Unless the Lord watches over the city,
>> the watcher stays awake in vain.
> It is in vain that you rise up early
>> and go late to rest (Ps 127:1-2a).

Antithetical parallelism is repetition of opposite terms or sentiments in which two lines contrast with one another. In the following examples the antithetical terms appear first at the beginning of the lines, then at the ends of the lines, and finally in a special crisscross pattern where the beginning of the first line antithetically matches the end of the second line and the middle of the first line antithetically matches the beginning of the second.

> May our sons in their youth
>> be like plants full grown,
> our daughters like corner pillars
>> cut for the structure of a palace (Ps 144:12).

> They will collapse and fall;
>> but we shall rise and stand upright! (Ps 20:8).

> The Lord preserves all who love [God];
>> but all the wicked [God] will destroy (Ps 145:20).

Making the lightnings with the rain;
Bringing forth the wind out of his treasures.
For full discussion, see Robert Lowth, *Isaiah: A New Translation; with a Preliminary Dissertation, and Notes Critical, Philological, and Explanatory* (orig. published in 1778; London: W. Baynes and Son, 1825) 23.

The special arrangement of the oppositions in the last example of antithetical parallelism in which (A) God preserves and (A') God destroys, with the contrast between (B) those who love God and (B') those who are wicked is called a chiastic pattern. Patterns of this sort repeat the parallel terms in reverse A-B-B'-A' order.

Chiastic patterns can contain any number of elements. Some chiastic patterns contain a climax in the very center of the pattern: A-B-C-D-C-B-A. Psalm 117 is structured as a simple A-B-A' chiastic pattern in which synonymously parallel terms appear in the A and B segments, while A' repeats in an abbreviated fashion the opening of the poem. God's steadfastness and faithfulness is exposed as the central B element in the pattern:

(A) **Praise the LORD, all nations!**
   Extol [God], all peoples!
(B) For great is [God's] steadfast love toward us;
   and the faithfulness of the LORD endures for ever.
(A') **Praise the LORD!**

Numerical patterns also appear in Hebrew poetry. Psalm 29 is a prayer which opens with a three-fold call to "ascribe to the LORD" glorious worship (see vv. 1-2). The motivation for this worship is then described in a seven-fold repetition of manifestations of "the voice of the LORD" before which all can but cry, "Glory!" (see vv. 3, 4, 5, 7, 8, 9). Three and seven usually suggest the idea of perfection or completeness. Four is also a special sacred number, doubtless because of the four compass directions.

Alphabetic arrangements called acrostic patterns organize the structure of some of the psalms. See for example, Psalms 9–10, 25, 34, 37, 111, 112, 119, 145. In English translations these alphabetic arrangements can only be discerned from the annotations that accompany the texts. In the case of Psalm 119, which is the longest psalm in the entire Psalter, annotated notes usually indicate that the length of this psalm is a result of a highly artificial structure in which each successive eight lines of poetry begin with successive letters of the Hebrew alphabet.

The point of all this is that when the psalmists pour out their life story to God they do so with freedom, extravagance, attentiveness to compositional detail, and all the excesses allowed by Hebrew poetry. Highly structured, intricately patterned literary forms are often vehicles for expression of a variety of emotions. Mountaintop experiences are celebrated with abandon. Experiences in the sorrowful depths of human existence are mourned without restraint. In the psalms, the human spirit gives voice to a range of emotions more intense than those encountered in everyday language. Poetry permits the psalmists to speak of God, others, themselves and their life experiences in words which strain the limits of human language. Poetry is not literal, not matter-of-fact, not straightforward.

Where but in poetry can "mountains skip like rams and hills like lambs" (Ps 114:4, 6)? Where but in poetry could it be imagined that "the meadows clothe themselves with flocks, the valleys deck themselves with grain, they shout and sing together for joy" (Ps 65:13)? Where but in poetry can a male become pregnant: "Behold, the wicked man conceives evil, and is pregnant with mischief, and brings forth lies" (Ps 7:14)? Where but in poetry can God ride a cherub on "the wings of the wind" (Ps 18:10)? Indeed, where but in poetry can any language for God be found?

Ordinary and extraordinary experiences of life catch the light and bring new perspectives into focus in the prayers of the psalmists. There is an elegance, innocence, dignity, and passionate, paradoxical excess in these prayers that calls for notice. Poetry allows prayer to escape literal language and to embrace logical opposites.

The psalmists are unafraid to stand with God and to ponder their life experiences closely. The psalmists look unflinchingly at their lives. They surrender to God their good times and their bad times. Their prayers reflect an attitude of trust that all life experiences are appropriate topics of conversation with God. What the superscriptions suggest and the words of the psalmists confirm is that everyday experiences are the stuff of poetry and prayer. Everyday experiences disclose the Holy.

The psalmists did not fashion what we have called hymns, enthronement psalms, songs of Zion, laments, prayers of thanksgiving and trust, royal psalms, liturgical psalms, wisdom psalms, or any of the mixed type psalms by accident. The original shaping of the prayers as religious poems and the process of the collection, refinement, and elaboration of the original prayers testify to the intentionality of the psalms. The psalmists mean what they say, whether their words delight or offend our sensibilities.

Ultimately, the poetic language of prayer is the language of self-surrender carefully considered. Praise and complaint are given over to God in these prayers in expressions spoken with full intentionality. Belief, trust, and hope in the covenant empower the psalmists to speak to and about God in powerful, poetic images.

In the next chapter we will examine the co-existence in the Psalter of prayers that arose from within the religious-political establishment and prayers that express estrangement from the establishment. Some prayers poetically maintain structure-legitimating theology and the belief that because God is present all is well with the world. Other prayers poetically challenge the legitimacy of these structures by protesting that because God is absent the world is in chaotic disarray.

For now, let us consider Thomas Merton's word to poets:

> We are not persuaders. We are children of the Unknown. We are the ministers of silence that is needed to cure all victims of absurdity who lie dying of a contrived joy. Let us then recognize ourselves for who we are: dervishes mad with secret therapeutic love which cannot be bought or sold, and which the politician fears more than violent revolution, for violence changes nothing. But love changes everything.
>
> We are stronger than the bomb.
>
> Let us now say "yes" to our own nobility by embracing the insecurity and abjection that a dervish existence entails.
>
> In the Republic of Plato there was already no place for poets and musicians, still less for dervishes and monks. As for the technological Platos who think they now run the world we live in, they imagine they can tempt us with banalities and abstractions. But we can elude them merely by stepping into the Heraklitean river which is never crossed twice.
>
> When the poet puts his foot in that ever-moving river, poetry itself is born out of the flashing water. In that unique instant, the truth is manifest to all who are able to receive it.
>
> No one can come near the river unless he walks on his own feet. He cannot come there carried in a vehicle.
>
> No one can enter the river wearing the garments of public and collective ideas. He must feel the water on his skin. He must know that immediacy is for naked minds only, and for the innocent.
>
> Come, dervishes: here is the water of life. Dance in it.[7]

[7] Merton, "Message to Poets," 160–61.

The language of prayer requires the heart of a poet. To pray is to dance in the water of life, to see God's light reflected in and through our lives. Truths communicated through ordinary or extraordinary life experiences are made known to those who dare to catch sight of themselves in God's light and walk into this water. Prayer is born of the words of our life-poem. The encounter of prayer is like the experience of water and light on *our* naked skin. The psalms bid us to consider our lives and its patterns with the eyes of a poet. With extravagant language and imagery we are invited to voice our understandings of God, self, and community in conversation with God. The Holy One bids us to take up our inheritance of faith by wading into the life-giving stream and seeing the Spirit's light refracted in our lives. We go with the language of poetry[8] and the disposition of the psalms that instruct us to pray from the particularity of our life experiences, whatever they may be. In prayer, we are all poets.

> The psalms are part of the world's greatest inheritance of enduring poetry. In these poems, humanity is set in the midst of a world that is unmistakably real and solid. It is described in ways that speak not merely to the mind but to all the senses. But it does more than depict the outer world; it explores the inner one. We are led psalm by psalm, line by line, to join hands across the gulf of time with the authors of these poems. What they were is what we are.[9]

---

[8] Much more could be said about the language of poetry and interested readers are urged to consult Patrick D. Miller, Jr., *Interpreting the Psalms* (Philadelphia: Fortress Press, 1986). His chapter "Poetry and Interpretation" and the sources he sites are most instructive.

[9] Chad Walsh, *A Rich Feast: Encountering the Bible* (New York: Harper & Row, 1981) 13.

Is it not better to pray for vengeance
than to take vengeance?
Walter Harrelson[1]

3

Anger and Praise

The psalms contain both inspiring and shocking poetic expressions of individual and communal concerns, perceptions, and exchanges with God. Some psalms verbalize positive experiences;
others voice negative concerns, perceptions, and exchanges.
There are, as we saw in Chapter 1, many more laments than
hymns of praise. In Chapter 2, we tried to recognize some of the
implications of the fact that poetry is the language of prayer in
the Psalter. Most psalms take ordinary, real experiences as beginning points of dialogue with God. Since there are so many
negative expressions in the psalms that we regularly skip over
in Lectionary selections of the psalms and hymns drawn from
the Psalter, it seems important in this chapter for us to look closely
at expressions of anger in the Book of Psalms.

Poetic freedom allows the psalmists to speak of God, others,
and themselves in unrestrained ways. The preponderance of laments in the Psalter suggests that feelings of anger are accepted
as appropriate starting points of prayers intended to change patterns of relationship with God, selves, and others. The psalmists
are unafraid to state clearly how they feel. They unambiguously
communicate to God the conflicts of their lives. There is something thoughtful and deliberate about the poetry of the laments
that makes their negativity terribly uncomfortable for many of

---

[1] Walter Harrelson, *Interpreting the Old Testament*, 416.

43

us. Yet I suspect that one of the corollaries of anger as it is expressed in the psalms is a corresponding belief that prayer changes things. The psalmists do not simply ventilate anger; they pray for change.

Our liturgical practices suggest that we are more comfortable with positive expressions about God and the world. An outsider observing one of our American services of worship might understandably come away thinking that we are a people whose lives are not plagued by any sort of negativity or disharmony. For the most part, we reject and disapprove of anger, particularly in worship. We act in composed, recollected, controlled ways. While we admit personal guilt and self-doubt in statements like "O Lord *I* am not worthy," we carefully limit expression of "anger" to remorse over our own shortcomings. Virtually the only change we pray for is change in ourselves. Even though the psalms include verses like those that follow, according to the Lectionary, we never use such verses in worship:

> Break the arm of the wicked and evildoers;
>   seek out their wickedness until you find none (Ps 10:15).

> Let all those be put to shame and confusion who seek
>   to snatch away my life;
> let those be turned back and brought to dishonor who
>   desire my hurt (Ps 40:14-15).

> Rise up, O judge of the earth;
>   give to the proud what they deserve! (Ps 94:2).

> O that you would kill the wicked, O God,
>   and that the bloodthirsty would depart from me (Ps 139:19).

Instead of negative sentiments like these just quoted, the Lectionary excerpts verses from these very same psalms that bespeak and encourage gentler, more moderate attitudes:

> ℟. **Do not forget the poor, O Lord!**
> You do see, for you behold misery and sorrow,
>   taking them in your hands.
> On you the unfortunate man depends;
>   of the fatherless you are the helper (Ps 10:14).[2]

---

[2] *Lectionary for Mass* (New York: Catholic Book Publishing Co., 1970) 395.

℟. **Here am I, Lord; I come to do your will.**
I have waited, waited for the Lord,
    and he stooped toward me and heard my cry.
And he put a new song into my mouth,
    a hymn to our God (Ps 40:1, 3).[3]

℟. **Happy the man you teach, O Lord.**
For the Lord will not cast off his people,
    nor abandon his inheritance;
But judgment shall again be with justice,
    and all the upright of heart shall follow it (Ps 94:14-15).[4]

℟. **You have searched me and you know me, Lord.**
O Lord, you have probed me and you know me;
    you know when I sit and when I stand;
    you understand my thoughts from afar.
My journeys and my rest you scrutinize,
    with all my ways you are familiar (Ps 139:1-3).[5]

This last psalm is a particularly instructive example. The Lectionary cites Psalm 139 seven times, quoting verses 1-3 six times, adding various other verses,[6] but always omitting the expressions of anger directed at God and against others in the psalm. The Lectionary uses only the italicized portion of the following text of Psalm 139, ignoring vv. 15-21, the verses that ask God to kill the wicked and include the word that the psalmist hates those who hate God with perfect hatred.

> *O LORD, you have searched me and known me!*
> *You know when I sit down and when I rise up;*
>   *you discern my thoughts from far away.*
> *You search out my path and my lying down,*
>   *and you are acquainted with all my ways.*
> *Even before a word is on my tongue,*
>   *O LORD, you know it completely.*
> *You hem me in, behind and before,*
>   *and lay your hand upon me.*

[3] Thirteen times this verse is quoted in the *Lectionary*, 65, 66, 121, 307, 314, 318, 422, 444, 474, 545, 786, 808, 918. Never is the negativity of vv. 14-15 anywhere expressed.

[4] See the *Lectionary*, 336, 392, 484.

[5] See the *Lectionary*, 426, 427, 440, 460, 462, 491, 587.

[6] The exception in the seven citations listed above in note 5 is on 427.

Such knowledge is too wonderful for me;
   it is so high that I cannot attain it.

Where can I go from your spirit?
   Or where can I flee from your presence?
If I ascend to heaven, you are there;
   if I make my bed in Sheol, you are there.
If I take the wings of the morning and
   settle at the farthest limits of the sea,
even there your hand shall lead me,
   and your right hand shall hold me fast.
If I say, "Surely the darkness shall cover me,
   and the light around me become night,"
even the darkness is not dark to you;
   the night is as bright as the day,
for darkness is as light to you.

For it was you who formed my inward parts;
   you knit me together in my mother's womb.
I praise you, for I am fearfully and wonderfully made.
Wonderful are your works; that I know very well.
   My frame was not hidden from you,
   when I was being made in secret,
      intricately woven in the depths of the earth.
Your eyes beheld my unformed substance,
      In your book were written all the days that were
      formed for me, when none of them as yet existed.
How weighty to me are your thoughts, O God!
      How vast is the sum of them!
I try to count them—they are more than the sand;
   I come to the end—I am still with you.

O that you would kill the wicked, O God,
   and that the bloodthirsty would depart from me—
those who speak of you maliciously,
   and lift themselves up against you for evil!
Do I not hate those who hate you, O Lord?
And do I not loathe those who rise up against you?
I hate them with perfect hatred;

   I count them my enemies.
Search me, O God, and know my heart;
   test me and know my thoughts.
See if there is any wicked way in me,
   and lead me in the way everlasting.

Unless we happen to know the entire text of a psalm, we might never suspect that the psalmists said angry words to God from the excerpts we use liturgically. It is simply a fact that the Lectionary and our culture discourage awareness and expression of anger. The psalms, on the other hand, do not. Negative and positive expressions stand in the psalms without the kind of editing to which we are accustomed in the Lectionary.

To be sure, the psalms do include descriptions of the world as well-ordered and sustained by a God whose continuing care for the earth and its inhabitants is a cause of wonder. Such psalms contain positive declarations like those in which self can say to self: "Bless the LORD, O my soul! O LORD my God, you are very great" (Ps 104:1). In public, a psalmist can proclaim: "This is the day which the LORD has made; let us rejoice and be glad in it" (Ps 118:24). Out of positive experiences, the community can declare: "We have thought on your steadfast love, O God, in the midst of your temple. As your name, O God, so your praise reaches to the ends of the earth" (Ps 48:9-10).

More often, however, the psalms tell of a world gone awry, twisted askew by God's absence, the triumph of enemies, or personal sin. In pain and distress, the psalmist can cry out:

> My God, my God, why have you forsaken me?
> Why are you so far from helping me,
>   from the word of my groaning?
> O my God, I cry by day, but you do not answer;
>   and by night, but find no rest (Ps 22:1-2).

Feeling abandoned, the community can protest:

> We have heard with our ears, O God,
>   our ancestors have told us,
>   what deeds you performed in their days,
>   in the days of old. . . .
> Yet you have cast us off and abased us,
>   and have not gone out with our armies.
> You have made us turn back from the foe;
>   and our enemies have gotten spoil.
> You have made us like sheep for the slaughter,
>   and scattered us among the nations. . . .

> All this has come upon us,
>> though we have not forgotten you,
>> or been false to your covenant. . . .
> Rouse yourself! Why do you sleep, O Lord?
>> Awake! Do not cast us off for ever! (Ps 44:1, 9-11, 17, 23).

A repentant sinner can pray: "Have mercy on me, O God, according to your steadfast love; according to your abundant mercy blot out my transgressions" (Ps 51:1).

Exaltation or shame, gladness or sadness, conviction that God is present or conviction that God is absent are all moments of *tehillim*, "praise" of God in the psalms. Positive and negative life experiences exist side by side as valid expressions of covenant. Shame and anger are not in any way disapproved or denied. The psalmists go to God as they are, not as we might think they ought to be.

Courageous choice of direction and movement toward divine-human congruity overrides the seeming contradiction of words from times of well-being as well as words from times of frustration. All seasons of life call for responsible surrender to the requirements of the covenant. Variety of experience is part of the pattern of prayer in the Psalter. No prayer seems to be ruled inappropriate.

Hymnic expressions of praise provide well-ordered maps of life that support belief in "God's non-negotiable governance"[7] of the world. Expressions of anger and frustration confront God with a need for negotiated change. Some psalms express the conviction that life is good and worthy of maintenance just as it is. Others protest the inequities of life with a passion that insists on change. The canon has room for both.

The faith expressed in the psalms supports and legitimates God's order as manifested in social, political, and religious structures. This same faith also boldly challenges and judges intolerable the disorder of God's world as manifested in these same structures. The incongruities of these various orientations to life and God are seemingly not troublesome to the psalmists. Hymns of celebration and the psalms of lament have simply found a place side by side. One is not presented as better than the other;

---

[7] Walter Brueggemann, "A Shape for Old Testament Theology, II: Embrace of Pain," *Catholic Biblical Quarterly* 47:3 (July 1985) 395.

they are simply different expressions of *tehillim,* praises of God. The psalms allow for both the maintenance of prevailing order and the call for its reorganization. Discernment belongs to prayer.

Examination of our own personal and communal prayers suggests that it is more difficult for us than it was for the psalmists to allow prayer to embrace negative experiences. We are generally at ease with expressions that celebrate, support, and legitimate the structures of our reality. But our public prayers, at least, underscore the fact that we are uncomfortable with expressions about God, community, self, or church that are fraught with anger and frustration. Many of us make a deliberate effort to control or change whatever it is inside ourselves that is at odds with the structures of our reality. For some of us our basic religious orientation has little room for the disorientation of resentment and anger. We act out of the belief that faithful people don't say hateful words, much less pray hateful words, and that rage is inappropriate, especially in prayer. Prayers become well-mannered words to God. So accustomed are some of us to permitting ourselves to say only "nice" things that we do not even recognize our rage. Others of us recognize our anger but believe that we need to put it aside when we talk to God. The lesson that the psalms teach is that anger is not evil or sinful. It is not something to overcome or fear. Anger is simply one of the subjects the faithful take to God in prayer.

Harriet Goldhor Lerner has written a guide about anger from a psychotherapeutic perspective. Her comments are helpful to our discussion:

> Thus, we too learn to fear our own anger, not only because it brings about the disapproval of others, but also because it signals the necessity for change. We may begin to ask ourselves questions that serve to block or invalidate our own experience of anger: "Is my anger legitimate?" "Do I have a right to be angry?" "What's the use of my getting angry?" "What good will it do?" These questions can be excellent ways of silencing ourselves and shutting off our anger.
>
> Let us question these questions. Anger is neither legitimate nor illegitimate, meaningful nor pointless. Anger simply is. To ask, "Is my anger legitimate?" is similar to asking, "Do I have a right to be thirsty?" After all, I just had a glass of water fifteen minutes ago. Surely my thirst is not legitimate. And be-

sides, what's the point of getting thirsty when I can't get anything to drink now, anyway?''

Anger is something we feel. It exists for a reason and always deserves our respect and attention. We all have a right to *everything* we feel—and certainly our anger is no exception.[8]

Expression of anger allows the psalmists to become agents of change in their relationship to God, self, and others. No matter what its cause, anger is not suppressed in the psalms; it is surrendered to God. From the psalmists we learn that God stands ready to hear all we need to say. The laments clearly show that the psalmists speak their angers and resentments with no reservations.

With regard to the very important distinction between angry prayers and violent actions, Harrelson says:

It is difficult to overestimate the importance of these laments. Viewed simply from the standpoint of the community's mental health, we can see how important it was that the community could address its laments and prayers to Yahweh without holding back its true feelings. Yahweh was ready, in their view, to hear their protestations. They could turn to Yahweh and state the simple facts of their experience. Yahweh might or might not come immediately to their aid, but at any rate nothing prevented them from saying exactly what they thought of Yahweh's governance of the universe. . . . Hatred of our enemies is a basic element in human life. These psalmists did not, as we generally do, hide their hatred from the deity in their prayers. Is it not of much greater import to pray to God for vengeance against our enemies than to take vengeance into our own hands?[9]

Of particular trouble for many interpreters are those vengeful prayers that are described as "imprecatory psalms." These prayers invoke God because of a particular experience of calamity and petition God to judge and punish the enemy harshly. About twenty psalms contain imprecatory elements,[10] and nine

[8] Harriet Goldhor Lerner, *The Dance of Anger* (New York: Harper & Row, Publishers, 1985) 3–4.

[9] Walter Harrelson, *Interpreting the Old Testament*, 415.

[10] See for instance, Pss 5:10; 10:15; 21:8-12; 28:4-5; 40:14-15; 52:5; 55:9-11; 68:2, 30; 94:2; 104:35; 139:19-22.

of these focus almost entirely on calling God to afflict evildoers. Psalms 7, 35, 58, 59, 69, 83, 109, 137, and 140 are imprecatory psalms that pray to God for the destruction or doom of others.

"O God, break the teeth in their mouths" is an exemplary imprecation (Ps 58:6). "Pour out your indignation upon them, and let your burning anger overtake them" (Ps 69:24) calls God to execute angry punishment. Included in Psalm 83 is a prayer that the enemies become like "dung for the ground" (Ps 83:10). Psalm 137 prays, "Happy shall he be who takes your little ones and dashes them against the rock!" (Ps 137:9). Psalm 140 asks for God's protection from wicked, violent enemies with the petition, "Let burning coals fall upon them! Let them be cast into pits, no more to rise!" (Ps 140:10). But most terrible of all is Psalm 109 in which an accused man begs God:[11]

> Appoint a wicked man against him;
>   let an accuser bring him to trial.
> When he is tried, let him come forth guilty;
>   let his prayer be counted as sin!
> May his days be few;
>   may another seize his goods!
> May his children be fatherless,
>   and his wife a widow!
> May his children wander about and beg;
>   may they be driven out of the ruins they inhabit!
> May the creditor seize all that he has;
>   may strangers plunder the fruits of his toil!
> Let there be none to extend kindness to him,
>   nor any to pity his fatherless children!
> May his posterity be cut off;
>   may his name be blotted out in the second generation!
> May the iniquity of his fathers be remembered before
>   the LORD,
>   and let not the sin of his mother be blotted out!
> Let them be before the LORD continually;
>   and may his memory be cut off from the earth!

[11] Vv. 6-19 are sometimes interpreted as a quotation of the charge spoken against the psalmist. I take these verses as the psalmist's own prayer for vengeance. The text can with good cause be interpreted in both ways. For summary of the various supporting arguments, see Leslie C. Allen, *Psalms 101–150*, Word Biblical Commentary 21 (Waco, TX: Word Books, 1983) 72–73.

> For he did not remember to show kindness,
>   but pursued the poor and the needy
>   and the brokenhearted to their death.
> He loved to curse; let curses come on him!
>   He did not like blessing; may it be far from him!
> He clothed himself with cursing as his coat,
>   may it soak into his body like water,
>   like oil into his bones!
> May it be like a garment which he wraps round him,
>   like a belt with which he daily girds himself!
>
> May this be the reward of my accusers from the LORD,
>   of those who speak evil against my life!
> But you, O God my Lord,
>   deal on my behalf for your name's sake;
>   because your steadfast love is good, deliver me! (Ps 109:6-21).

These violent, vengeful sentiments may be embarrassments to our religious sensitivities, but they are not censored or silenced in the psalms. Negative wishes are spoken with the hope that God will execute swift, harsh judgment against the offenders. The psalmists do not sanitize their fierce desire for strict retribution. They pray for what they want. They express their bitterness and vindictiveness with the promise that once their own righteousness and God's justice are proven, they will praise their deliverance and God's sovereignty. Stuhlmueller suggests that imprecations are "almost like a valve to release pressure, a healthy way of controlling anger."[12]

The attitude of the psalmists that God is the avenger is of particular importance in understanding what at first glance looks like unrestrained vindictiveness in the imprecatory psalms. Rage is not pent up in the psalms. In prayer, rage is relinquished to God. It is God who decides how vengeance is to be executed. Brueggemann points out that:

> When God is able to say, "Vengeance is mine" (Deut. 32:35; Rom. 12:19), it implies, "not yours." The submitting partner is no longer free to take vengeance. . . . So the submission is an unburdening and freeing from pettiness and paralysis for praise and thanksgiving.[13]

[12] Stuhlmueller, *Psalms 1*, 313.
[13] Brueggemann, *The Message of the Psalms*, 86.

In discussing how Psalm 109 might be appropriated in the life of faith, Brueggemann says:

> I suggest that we had best begin with an acknowledgment of the reality of vengeance. There may be some who are not keen on vengeance because life is lived in suppressed discipline. For others life has gone so well that this psalm may not be for them. But for the rest, this psalm deals in realism. It knows about the unfairness and exploitation that evoke rage. It knows that such rage is tenacious and will be expressed and not denied. It knows that the rage is rightly carried even to the presence of Yahweh, whose rule is marked by majesty, faithfulness, and compassion.[14]

In sum, the psalms teach that prayer changes things and that all life experience must be brought before God. Anger is not to be ignored, or eliminated, or stored up. Angry people are not driven from the community. As covenant partners, all are called to submit their lives to God and to relinquish unto God in real and irreversible ways the governance of the universe and their corner in it. The psalms teach that our part in the process is to risk a journey on a path whose destination we will know only in dialogue with God. Along the way we may encounter experiences that cause celebration or we may encounter experiences that cause anger. No matter. We are called to offer—to give up—our anger and our joy to a God who is with us, ever ready to hear our praises.[15]

Unfortunately, we have lost the practice of unrestrained expression of rage in prayer. The sad corollary to this truth is that we may also have lost the attitude that vengeance belongs only to God. Some have learned consciously, others unconsciously, to hold on to the suppressed vengeance that seethes inside them. Others practice it against family or friends. Nation rises up against nation. Regrettably, our actions speak louder than the words we

---

[14] Ibid., 85.

[15] For additional information about anger and prayer, see Sheila Carney, "God Damn God: A Reflection on Expressing Anger in Prayer," *Biblical Theology Bulletin* 13:4 (October 1983) 116–120. J. Carl Laney, "A Fresh Look at the Imprecatory Psalms," *Bibliotheca Sacra* (January–March 1981) 35–45. Carol P. Christ, "Expressing Anger at God: An Essay in Story Theology," *Anima* 5:3-10. Elizabeth R. Skoglund, *To Anger, With Love* (New York: Harper & Row, Publishers, 1977).

refuse to say to God. Our individual and societal actions show
that we need to learn about anger and what to do with it.

According to the 1970 *Lectionary for Mass*, on Thursday of the
thirtieth week of the year, we recite Psalm 109. Here in its entirety is the barely recognizable version of all that we permit ourselves to pray in our liturgy:

> R̈. **Save me, O Lord, in your kindness.**
> Do you, O God, my Lord, deal kindly with me
> > for your name's sake;
> > in your generous kindness rescue me;
> For I am wretched and poor,
> > and my heart is pierced within me.
>
> R̈. **Save me, O Lord, in your kindness.**
> Help me, O Lord, my God;
> > save me, in your kindness,
> And let them know that this is your hand;
> > that you, O Lord, have done this.
>
> R̈. **Save me, O Lord, in your kindness.**
> I will speak my thanks earnestly to the Lord,
> > and in the midst of the throng I will praise [God],
> For [God] stood at the right hand of the poor man,
> > to save him from those who would condemn him.
>
> R̈. **Save me, O Lord, in your kindness.**
> (Ps 109:21-22, 26-27, 30-31)

How helpful it might be to learn from the psalms to say and
really mean, "To you, O God of Holy Mystery, I lift up my whole
life in times of celebration as well as in times of frustration and
rage." Frustration and rage need to be identified, named, and
surrendered to God. Prayerful expression of anger is more than
an abstraction. It is the first step of the movement through anger
suggested by the psalmists' practice of relinquishing it to God
in prayer. The psalmists seem to know that if we would be free,
we must name who we are, where we stand, what we want, what
is and what is not acceptable to us. Wholeness and holiness require choice of direction, movement, and change from ways of
enslavement to ways of freedom. The psalms—if not the
Lectionary—teach us to tell the whole of our story to God, self,
and community.

Happy are those
who do not follow the advice of the wicked,
or take the path that sinners tread,
or sit in the seat of scoffers;
but delight in the law of YHWH and
meditate on God's law day and night.

Ps 1:1-2

4

Happiness and Prayer

The psalms give more attention to "happiness" than any other book in the Hebrew Bible. The very first word in the Book of Psalms is: "Happy" is the one who walks not in the counsel of the wicked, who delights in meditating on God's law day and night (Ps 1:1-2).[1] The Hebrew word 'ashre, which means "blessed, fortunate, happy," occurs twenty-six times in the psalms and only twenty times elsewhere in the entire Hebrew Bible.[2] The proportionately large number of occurrences of the word 'ashre in the psalms suggests that the psalmists thought it appropriate in conversation with God to identify and name what constitutes happiness for the individual, community, or nation. Examination of the instances of the word 'ashre in the psalms discloses that there is great variety in defining "happiness."

The following is a listing of all twenty-six occurrences of the

---

[1] Stuhlmueller maintains that the opening phrase of Ps 1 which is sometimes translated, "Blessed is that one," is better translated in a less liturgical way, "How happy that one." See his analysis of Ps 1, *Psalms 1*, as well as his helpful interpretation of all the individual psalms included in our discussion of "happiness." He rightly points out that 'ashre, "happy," (as distinguished from baruk, "blessed") is "closely connected with right living in one's daily life" (*Psalms 1*, 59).

[2] Pss 41:2 and 72:17 contain verbal forms of 'shr meaning "to pronounce happy or blessed." These forms will be discussed more fully in this chapter.

55

word *'ashre*, a Hebrew plural noun[3] that is used only in its construct form in the Book of Psalms:

Ps 1:1	Happy is the one who has not followed the counsel of the wicked
Ps 2:12	Happy are all who take refuge in [God]
Ps 32:1	Happy is the one whose transgression is forgiven
Ps 32:2	Happy the one whom YHWH does not hold guilty
Ps 33:12	happy the nation whose God is YHWH
Ps 34:8	happy the one who takes refuge in [God]
Ps 40:4	happy is the one who makes YHWH his trust
Ps 41:1	Happy is the one who is thoughtful of the wretched
Ps 65:4	happy is the one whom you choose and invite to dwell in your courts
Ps 84:4	Happy are those who dwell in your house
Ps 84:5	happy is the man who finds refuge in you
Ps 84:12	happy is the one who trusts in you
Ps 89:15	happy the people who know the joyful shout
Ps 94:12	happy is the one whom you discipline, O YHWH
Ps 106:3	happy are those who act justly
Ps 112:1	happy is the one who fears YHWH
Ps 119:1	happy are those whose way is blameless
Ps 119:2	happy are those who observe [God's] decrees
Ps 127:5	happy is the man who fills his quiver with them (sons)
Ps 128:1	happy are all who fear YHWH
Ps 128:2	you shall be happy and you shall prosper (when your wife is like a fruitful vine and your children are like olive shoots around your table)
Ps 137:8	happy shall anyone be who repays you in kind what you have inflicted on us
Ps 137:9	happy shall anyone be who seizes your babies and shatters them against the rocks
Ps 144:15a	happy the people who have it so (prosperity)
Ps 144:15b	happy the people whose God is YHWH
Ps 146:5	happy is the one who is helped by the God of Jacob

---

[3] According to the standard Hebrew-English dictionary (Francis Brown, S. R. Driver, and Charles A. Briggs, *A Hebrew and English Lexicon of the Old Testament* [Oxford: Clarendon, 1975], 80), *'ashre* is presumably masculine, though the gender of this noun is not clearly exhibited in Hebrew.

Tabulation of like expressions by individuals, the community, and the nation demonstrates the varied definitions of "happy" in the psalms. No more than two verses identify "happy" identically. All the verses define "happiness" as something known in the doing or in the having it done to you or for you. "Happiness" is not an abstract concept; it is a real, identifiable experience.

"HAPPY" IS THE ONE

—who avoids the wicked and delights in God's law (Ps 1:1-2)
—who fears YHWH and delights in God's commandments (Ps 112:1)
—who trusts YHWH (Pss 40:4; 84:12)
—whose sin is forgiven (Ps 32:1)
—whose help is the God of Jacob (Ps 146:5)
—who takes refuge in God (Ps 34:8)
—whom God chooses to dwell in the temple (Ps 65:4)
—whom God chastens (Ps 94:12)
—who considers the poor (Ps 41:1)
—who has a quiver full of sons (Ps 127:5)
—who requites you with what you have done to us (Ps 137:8)
—who dashes your little ones against the rocks (Ps 137:9)

"HAPPY" ARE THEY

—who take refuge in God (Ps 2:11b)
—who dwell in God's house (Ps 84:4)
—whose strength is in God (Ps 84:5)
—who know the festal shout (Ps 89:15)
—who do justice (Ps 106:3)
—whose way is blameless, who walk in the law of YHWH (Ps 119:1)
—who keep God's testimonies (Ps 119:2)
—who fear YHWH (Ps 128:1, 2)
—to whom blessings fall (Ps 144:15)
—whose God is YHWH (Ps 144:15)

"HAPPY" IS THE NATION

—whose God is YHWH (Ps 33:12)

"Happiness" is a relational experience.[4] Individuals or the community define what it means to be blessed, fortunate, or happy in concrete terms of desired associations or experiences of connectedness. Most often in the psalms "happiness" has to do with being in right relationship with God. Sometimes "happiness" has to do with the high regard of onlookers. And in the case of Psalm 137, "happiness" has to do with exercise of vengeance and vindication. "Happiness" is poetically identified in a variety of ways in the Psalter. In all cases, those who pray bring to conscious expression what it is that they understand "happiness" to be. Daryl Schmidt points out that *'ashre* (and its Greek counterpart *makarios*, a word used regularly in the nine beatitudes in Matthew and the four in Luke) introduces the utterance or declaration of a blessing. He suggests that a good alternate English translation of *'ashre* that captures the plural form of the word is "Congratulations!"[5] This suggestion works well in some of the examples listed above, but not in all. Indeed *'ashre* does involve validation, sometimes from an external source but more often in the psalms from within the person who prays. Self could be un-

[4] In our discussion of this chapter and "happiness" in the Bible, Claudia Camp made the comment, "External recognition of this state is as important as internal feelings." She alerted me to Daryl D. Schmidt's article "Congratulations, You Poor!" *The Fourth R* 3:2 (March 1990):13-14, which makes a similar point in rendering the performative utterance or declaration of blessing in declarations introduced by the Hebrew *'ashre* and the Greek *makarios* with the word "congratulations!" Schmidt is working primarily with the beatitudes in Matthew and Luke and he rightly says, "We congratulate someone by saying 'Congratulations!' And only when someone says 'Congratulations!' is a person congratulated. That is the kind of performative language that can effectively translate the beatitudes. It grants someone recognition, usually for their good fortune, whether deserved or not. (It also happens to be plural like the Hebrew *ashre*.)" (14). So Schmidt translates, "Congratulations, poor people! God's kingdom is yours!" and "Congratulations, those now hungry! You'll be filled!" (14). In the beatitudes, Jesus is externally recognizing the state of the disenfranchised. In these cases, I agree that external recognition is significant validation. However, I do not find that all the psalms involve external recognition. The impulse in the psalms is often more self-identification, self-validation in conversation with God.
[5] Schmidt, 14.

derstood to say to self, "Congratulations for not following the counsel of the wicked!" (Ps 1:1). But "happy" works here equally well, in my estimation. Schmidt helpfully remarks that "happiness" is not to be confused with " 'Be-Happy Attitudes' suggesting a smiling face and a warm feeling."[6] Such indeed is the case in the psalms. No face smiles when the psalmist prays, "Happy is the one who requites you with what you have done to us!" (Ps 137:8).

Another word formed from the same Hebrew consonants as those in the word *'ashre*, "happy, blessed, fortunate," appears in feminine plural noun forms of *'ashur* in an additional six instances in the psalms. These feminine plural nouns are translated as "steps," which is a poetic figure of what might be characterized as a "happy" life. The six occurrences emphasize sureness of direction and right movement along God's way. The poetic image is most often of "steps" holding to the right path. Though we miss this equivalence in English translations because our word "steps" sounds nothing like our word "happiness," in Hebrew the similarities are readily observed.

In the following examples "steps" (*'ashur*), a word formed from Hebrew letters quite like those of "happy" (*'ashre*), are highlighted. In Hebrew, the sound resemblances in the examples evoke a connection between experiences of happiness and being on the right path. A life lived on the right path with "steps" taken in the right direction is a "happy" life.

Ps 17:5	My **steps** have held fast to your paths, my feet have not slipped.
Ps 17:11	Our **steps** tottered, they surrounded me, they fixed their eyes to cast me to the ground.
Ps 37:31	The law of his God is in his heart; his **steps** do not slip.
Ps 40:2	[God] drew me up from the desolate pit, out of the mud of the miry bog, and set my feet upon a rock; making my **steps** secure.
Ps 44:18	Our heart has not turned back, nor have our **steps** departed from your way.
Ps 73:2	But as for me, my feet had almost stumbled, my **steps** had well nigh slipped.

[6] Ibid., 13.

In addition, there are two verbal forms of *'shr* in the psalms. Both these verbs are formed of the same consonants as the word *'ashre*, "happy." In Psalm 41, a Pual Imperfect verb, "called happy," appears in v. 2, following the masculine plural noun "happy" in v. 1:

> Happy *('ashre)* is he who considers the poor!
> YHWH delivers him in the day of trouble;
> YHWH protects him and keeps him alive;
> he is *called happy (ye'ushar)* in the land.

In Ps 72:17, a Piel Imperfect form of the verb appears:

> May they bless themselves by him,
> all nations *call him happy (ye'ashruhu)!*

The important thing about "happiness" in the psalms is that it is identified as a concrete experience and named in prayer. "Happiness" involves the freedom to identify desires in God's presence and to take steps that lead straight along God's way. Individual or communal determination of exactly what "happiness" is depends on the life circumstances of those making the decision. "Happiness" is not static or fixed by one commonly held definition. It is a dynamic, relational state to be discerned in prayer.

Closely related to this discernment of what constitutes individual or communal happiness is decision about choice of direction. The psalmists know when they have nearly strayed from God's path, even as they know when they are "happy." The individual and the community start from where their feet are planted, so to speak. "Happiness" involves choice of direction and movement toward increased divine-human congruence. In dialogue with God, the psalmists find their way on God's path. "Happy" indeed is the one on the right path, whose steps do not slip or stray.

The twenty-six occurrences of the plural Hebrew noun *'ashre* (blessed, fortunate, happy) in the psalms stand in comparison with only twenty other references to this same word "happy" in the rest of the Hebrew Bible. Four of these occurrences appear in judgments of the Queen of Sheba who declares Solomon's wives and attendants "happy" because of their continual proximity to Solomon's wisdom (twice in 1 Kgs 10:8; twice in 2 Chr

9:7). Eight uses of "happy" appear in Proverbs: "happy" is the one who finds wisdom (Prov 3:13); who keeps wisdom's ways (Prov 8:32) and listens to wisdom's instruction (Prov 8:34); who is kind to the poor (Prov 14:21); who trusts YHWH (Prov 16:20); who fears YHWH always (Prov 28:14); who keeps the law (Prov 29:18); and "happy" are the children of the righteous (Prov 20:7).

In Genesis, Leah names the second son of Jacob and her maid Zilpah, "Asher," saying, "Happy am I! For the women will call me happy" (Gen 30:13). Just before his death, Moses blesses the tribes, "Happy are you, O Israel! Who is like you, a people saved by YHWH, the shield of your help, and the sword of your triumph!" (Deut 33:29). In the Book of Job, Eliphaz says, "Happy is the one whom God reproves" (Job 5:17). Ecclesiastes includes the maxim, "Happy are you, O land, when your king is the son of free men, and your princes feast at the proper time, for strength, and not for drunkenness!" (Eccl 10:17). Isaiah declares "happy" all who wait for the Lord (Isa 30:18); who "sow beside all waters and let the feet of the ox and the ass range free" (Isa 32:20); "happy" is the one who keeps justice and does righteousness (Isa 56:2). Daniel's guide tells him, "Happy is the one who waits and comes to the thousand three hundred and thirty-five days" (Dan 12:12).

"Happiness" is as diverse an experience in these other biblical references as it is in the Book of Psalms. There is no biblical consensus about "happiness." What remains most remarkable is the proportionately large number of references in the psalms to "happiness." The psalmists clearly considered it appropriate to voice to God their individual and corporate understandings about "happiness." Prayer is seemingly the most fitting occasion to talk about "happiness." In dialogue with God, the psalmists show no restraint in identifying and naming precisely what they believe constitutes "happiness."

Since, as we saw in Chapter 1, wisdom psalms attend to issues involved in daily living and emphasize the choice of the way of righteousness over the way of wickedness, it is understandable that *'ashre* appears ten times in wisdom psalms (Pss 1:1; 32:1, 2; 34:8; 112:1; 119:1, 2; 127:5; 128:1, 2). Consideration of "happiness" fits well with consideration of contrasting life choices and their consequences. But *'ashre* also appears sixteen times in other psalm types, which implies that "happiness" belongs more generally to prayer as a whole than to wisdom psalms as an exclusive category.[7] Occurrences of *'ashre* appear three times in hymns of praise (Pss 33:12; 65:4; 146:5); three times in a Song of Zion (Ps 84:4, 5, 12); twice in a communal lament (Ps 137:8, 9); once in a royal psalm (Ps 2:12); once in a liturgy of divine protection (Ps 106:3); and six times in mixed type psalms (Pss 40:4; 41:1; 89:15; 94:12; 144:15a, b).

"Happy" not only appears across psalm types, but at strategic compositional points in the Book of Psalms as well. In Book I (Pss 1-41), *'ashre* appears in the book's opening and closing psalm (Pss 1:1 and 41:1). In Book III, *'ashre* appears in the book's closing psalm (Ps 89:15). In Book IV, *'ashre* also appears in the book's closing psalm (Ps 106:3). Occurrences of *'ashre* cluster most densely in Book I and Book V (Pss 107-150), acting like book ends to the collection as a whole. Eight of the twenty-six occurrences appear in Book I (Pss 1:1; 2:12; 32:1, 2; 33:12; 34:8; 40:4; 41:1). Eleven occurrences are found in Book V (Pss 112:1; 119:1, 2; 127:5; 128:1, 2; 137:8, 9; 144:15a, b; 146:5).

"Happy" appears six times in psalms that are themselves compositionally complex, notably the mixed type psalms (Pss 40:4; 41:1; 89:15; 94:12; 144:15a, b). Two of these mixed type prayers close Books (Psalm 41, Book I; Psalm 89, Book III). The particular conjunction of prayer types in these mixed type psalms serves to illustrate the fact that prayer is believed to effect real change. In Psalm 41, thanksgiving (vv. 1-3; 11-12) encircles a lament, which may originally have been an independent prayer (vv. 4-10). The request that God show "graciousness" to the psalmist (v. 4; v. 10) is not left as simply a petition. The structure of the psalm teaches by its didactic opening and closing surrounding the lament that the requested deliverance is realized.[8] The declaration that "happy" is the one who considers the poor because God delivers such a person in a day of trouble (v. 1) is proven factual by the testimony in vv. 11-12 that the individual knows that God is pleased because the enemy has not triumphed. While in most of the laments change is anticipated and hence only potential, in a psalm like this one that closes Book I, the psalmist knows

---

[7] In our discussion of "Wisdom Psalms" in Chapter 1, I listed Roland Murphy's helpful summary of eight characteristics of wisdom psalms. One of these is the appearance of the "blessed" (*'ashre*) formula. While it is true that ten occurrences of *'ashre* are found in wisdom psalms, not all appearances of *'ashre* signal a wisdom context. Sixteen other occurrences appear in other psalm types.

[8] For detailed treatment of Psalm 41, see Stuhlmueller, *Psalms 1*, 220-23.

that the lament did its work because the enemy did not triumph (compare v. 5 in the lament with v. 11 in the thanksgiving).

Book III ends similarly. Psalm 89 is an elaborate interlacing of hymn (vv. 1-8), oracle (vv. 19-37), and lament (vv. 38-52).[9] Confidence about the reality of God's steadfastness marks the assertion, "Happy are the people who know the festal shout, who walk, O Lord, in the light of your countenance" (v. 15). A comparable case can be made for the other mixed type psalms. In Psalm 40, confidence that "happy" is the one who trusts YHWH (v. 4) appears in the context of an individual thanksgiving prayer (vv. 1-11), which prefaces an individual lament (vv. 12-17). In Psalm 94, a national lament (vv. 1-15) that includes the declaration "happy" is the one whom God chastens (v. 12) is followed by a question that asks who stands up for the psalmist against evildoers (v. 16), which in turn is followed by a prayer of confidence (vv. 17-23). In large measure the juxtaposition of request or belief with confident assertion of deliverance in the mixed type psalms serves to teach that change does occur for those who pray.

Psalm 144 is as Stuhlmueller says, "a combination of parts that were not adequately blended together."[10] Individual lament, likely of a king (vv. 1-11) is followed by a "new song" of confident prayer for a prosperous year that ends with the declaration, "Happy the people to whom such blessings fall! Happy the people whose God is YHWH!" (v. 15). Even though the blending of the parts is not smooth, the complaint of the lament is mitigated by the confidence of the second part of the psalm. The proximity of the parts implies an attitude that prayer changes things.

The psalms suggest that "happiness" is available to those who pray. The conviction in many psalms is that God wants us to be "happy." The occurrences of *'ashre* hold out as an ideal the belief that "happiness" belongs to those who are straight with God. It is a striking fact that the practice of identifying "happiness" is more widespread in the Book of Psalms than anywhere else in the Hebrew Bible.

We began our discussion of those who prayed the psalms by saying that the psalmists do not present a systematic description of one right way to pray. We end by saying that "happiness"

[9] For further analysis, see Stuhlmueller, *Psalms 2*, 59–66.
[10] Ibid., 207.

is not one single, quantifiable concept for the psalmists. "Happiness" and prayer belong together in ways that suggest a predominantly optimistic orientation to God and life that undergirds the confident belief that things can change.

Since *'ashre*, the first word in the psalms, begins with *'aleph*, the first letter of the Hebrew alphabet, it is tempting to say that the ABC's of prayer start with naming what constitutes "happiness." From its start the Book of Psalms emphasizes that "happiness" involves being linked to God's way in ordinary, everyday life experiences. Stuhlmueller says it this way: "Ps 1 was clearly meant to be a coalescing force in the psalter and by its own secular contact to keep the prayer of Israel closely in touch with the total life of Israel and this life closely attached to God."[11]

In our times when appeals to "happiness" compete for our attention through societal, cultural, and even religious pressures, we might do well to heed the psalmists' practice of unrestrainedly expressing to God what we want from life and even from prayer. "Happy," indeed, are we who with the psalmists learn how to name what we really want and to pray poetic words of anger or praise out of the experiences of our daily lives. "Happy" are we who know which path is God's path for us. The prayers of the psalmists tell us much about the importance of choice of direction and movement along the right path. Covenant with God is a matter of life or death, of "happiness" or lamentable desolation.

Before we turn to discussion of who this covenant God is for the psalmists, seven things the psalms have taught about prayer call for summary:

1. Prayer comes out of lived experience.
2. All life experiences are appropriate subjects of conversation with God.
3. Laments and hymns praise God; both are *tehillim*.
4. The language of prayer is the language of poetry.
5. Anger can be relinquished to God in prayer.
6. Happiness can be rightly identified in prayer and experienced in a way of life that is God's way.
7. Prayer changes things.

Our examination of who the psalmists are shows that prayer fosters rectification and right living. In dialogue with God praise

[11] *Psalms 1*, 59.

is voiced, laments are expressed, anger is relinquished, thanksgiving and trust are spoken. In a real way, faith and honest words to God change the reality of the psalmists. The content of their conversations and the variety of attitudes of those who pray is less significant in the psalms than the dynamic belief, hope, and trust in the God of the covenant modeled in their prayers. Prayer changes those who pray in ways we can usually only sense. Prayer calls God to action. The way of prayer in the psalms allows new disclosure about who the individual or community is in relationship to God and who God is for them.

II. THE GOD OF THE PSALMISTS

Steadfast love and faithfulness will meet;
righteousness and peace will kiss each other.
Ps 85:10

5

Tradition and Conventions of Faith in the Psalms

Covenant is the foundation of all understandings of God and the basis of all prayers like those found in the Book of Psalms. Confidence in YHWH's graciousness and dependability is a hallmark of prayer. God is presumed sufficient to all needs, and the psalmists assume that God is or should be faithful to the covenant in good times and in bad. The psalmists virtually never struggle with the question of God's existence. They believe that God alleviated distress for their ancestors and that God will alleviate distress for them. When God is not present, the psalmist says, "My God, my God, why have you forsaken me?" (Ps 22:1). The psalmist depends on God's accessibility and saving presence:

You have said, "Seek my face."
  My heart says to you,
"Your face, YHWH, do I seek."
  Hide not your face from me.
Turn not your servant away in anger,
  you who have been my help.
Cast me not off, forsake me not,
  O God of my salvation!
For my father and my mother have forsaken me,
  but YHWH will take me up (Ps 27:8-10).

Biblical faith teaches that covenant begins with God's invitation to and participation in a life-giving and life-sustaining relationship that includes deliverance from present bondage and hope for the future. Prayer brings trust in this relational process into practice and focus. Trust is born of relational experience that permits the psalmists to depend upon the God of the covenant and to hope in a reality larger than self or community. Whether petition, praise, or thanksgiving motivates the prayer of the psalmists, trust in relationship with God undergirds their prayer. Some psalms express the positive attitudes that God is readily available, faithful, and constant. Others reflect negative experiences that God is unavailable, unfaithful, and not constant. Nonetheless, all the psalms assume that the covenant relationship is potentially a life-giving and life-sustaining resource. If covenant is negatively experienced, the psalmists seem to believe that the unfavorableness of whatever difficulty is affecting them can be changed.

Covenant is a theme that appears in a variety of ways in the psalms. Ps 25:10 expresses the positive sentiment that, "All the paths of YHWH are steadfast love and faithfulness, for those who keep [God's] covenant and testimonies." God "remembers" and shows abundant mercy to those who keep the covenant (Ps 106:45). God "provides food" and "sends redemption" on account of the covenant (Ps 111:5, 9). YHWH swears to David, "If your sons keep my covenant and my testimonies which I shall teach them, their sons also for ever shall sit upon your throne" (Ps 132:12).

Covenant is to be remembered and kept by the faithful *and* by God. Covenant is maintained by active doing of it. To "remember" God is to "do" covenant in such a way as to be rightly oriented in life or to regain balance:

> These things I remember,
>   as I pour out my soul:
> how I went with the throng,
>   and led them in procession to the house of God,
> with glad shouts and songs of thanksgiving,
>   a multitude keeping festival.
> Why are you cast down, O my soul,
>   and why are you disquieted within me?

Hope in God; for I shall again praise [God],
  my help and my God.
My soul is cast down within me, therefore I remember
  you from the land of Jordan and of Hermon,
    from Mount Mizar (Ps 42:4-6).

God, too, is charged to "remember" the covenant with the psalmist. "Remember your word to your servant, in which you have made me hope" (Ps 119:49). God is asked to "remember" a range of concerns, including offerings and burnt sacrifices (Ps 20:3), the congregation (Ps 74:2), the enemy who scoffs at the divine name (Ps 74:18, 22), the measure of what life is (Ps 89:47), how the servant is scorned and insulted (Ps 89:50), the psalmist who wants to be among those favored and delivered by God (Ps 106:4), all the hardships that David endured (Ps 132:1), and the sins of the Edomites against Jerusalem (Ps 137:7).

"Remembering" is a way of dealing with misery. When sleepless and troubled, one psalmist prays, "I remember the years long ago" (Ps 77:5) when you, O God, were steadfast and gracious, and "I will call to mind the deeds of YHWH, I will remember your wonders of old" (Ps 77:11). This act of remembering seems to give the psalmist hope that there will be a "way through the sea" (Ps 77:19). Active remembering of past experiences of God's mighty yet mysterious deliverance makes tolerable an otherwise unbearable situation of distress. Remembrance grounds hope that never suppresses or denies the reality of the psalmists, whether that reality be positive or negative. In Ps 143:5-6 the psalmist prays, "I remember the days of old, I meditate on all that you have done; I muse on what your hands have wrought. I stretch out my hands to you; my soul thirsts for you like a parched land."

Grateful recollection motivates the confident exhortation to the chosen ones in Ps 105:5: "Remember the wonderful works that [God] has done, [God's] miracles, and the judgments [God] uttered." And Ps 119:55 adds that remembering involves doing of the law: "I remember your name in the night, O YHWH, and keep your law."

"Not remembering" is disastrous in the psalms. "Let my tongue cleave to the roof of my mouth, if I do not remember you, if I do not set Jerusalem above my highest joy!" (Ps 137:6). The ancestors in Egypt got into terrible trouble that led to rebellion against the Most High at the Red Sea because "they did not remember" the abundance of God's love (Ps 106:7). The infamous wicked enemy of Psalm 109 is cursed because he "did not remember to show kindness, but pursued the poor and needy and the brokenhearted to their death" (Ps 109:16).

The psalmist whom *God* does not remember is "like one forsaken among the dead, like the slain that lie in the grave, like those whom you remember no more, for they are cut off from your hand" (Ps 88:5). Deliverance is at stake for the psalmist who prays, "Remember not the sins of my youth, or my transgressions; according to your steadfast love remember me, for your goodness' sake, O YHWH!" (Ps 25:7).

Steadfast love is available "to those who keep [God's] covenant and remember to do [God's] commandments" (Ps 103:18). Hope for the future is expressed by the psalmist who speaks of the time when, "All the ends of the earth shall remember and turn to YHWH; and all the families of the nations shall worship before [God]" (Ps 22:27). Indeed, an ideal time of peace is envisioned by the psalmist who proclaims the following oracle of assurance:

> Steadfast love and faithfulness will meet;
> righteousness and peace will kiss each other.
> Faithfulness will spring up from the ground,
> and righteousness will look down from the sky.
> Yea, YHWH will give what is good,
> and our land will yield its increase (Ps 85:10-12).

It is a violation of covenant for covenant members to conspire against each other or against God:

> My companion stretched out his hand against his friends,
> he violated his covenant (Ps 55:20).

> Their heart was not steadfast toward [God];
> they were not true to [God's] covenant (Ps 78:37).

> Yea, they conspire with one accord;
> against you they make a covenant (Ps 83:5).

Embedded in the four psalms, classified as "Judgment Liturgies" (Pss 50, 81, 82, 95),[1] are expressions of God's judgment

---

[1] See Chapter 1, Types of Prayer.

and/or protection of covenant members. Particularly noteworthy are the following examples in which God or a cultic official speaking for God says words of judgment to the people on account of the covenant:

> "Gather to me my faithful ones,
>> who made a covenant with me by sacrifice!"
>
> . . .
>
> "Hear, O my people, and I will speak,
> O Israel, I will testify against you.
> I am God, your God."
>
> . . .
>
> To the wicked God says:
> "What right have you to recite my statutes,
>> or take my covenant on your lips?
> For you hate discipline,
>> and you cast my words behind you" (Ps 50:5, 7, 16, 17).
>
> I am YHWH your God,
>> who brought you up out of the land of Egypt.
> Open your mouth wide, and I will fill it (Ps 81:10).
>
> Harden not your hearts, as at Meribah,
>> as on the day at Massah in the wilderness,
>> when your ancestors tested me,
>> and put me to the proof, though
>>> they had seen my work (Ps 95:8-9)

In other examples, the psalmists celebrate God's dependability on account of the covenant. In Ps 103:17-18, the psalmist asserts that "the steadfast love of YHWH is from everlasting to everlasting" for those "who keep the covenant and remember to do all the commandments." Ps 105:8-10 makes the claim that God is forever mindful of the "everlasting covenant" made with Abraham, Isaac, and Jacob.

Psalm 89 is a special prayer in which the psalmist remembers God's word that steadfast love belongs to the king forever as a "covenant that will stand firm" (vv. 1-4). In this prayer, God twice promises the anointed one steadfast love: "My steadfast love I will keep for him forever, and my covenant will stand firm for him" (Ps 89:28); "I will not violate my covenant or alter the word that went forth from my lips" (Ps 89:34). But another voice speaks against God in protest, "You have renounced the covenant with your servant; you have defiled his crown in the dust'' (Ps 89:39). Then God's faithfulness is put to question: ''Lord, where is your steadfast love of old, which by your faithfulness you did swear to David?'' (Ps 89:49). The prayer ends with God being called to ''remember'' the scorned yet faithful anointed servant (Ps 89:50-51).

This sentiment of charging God with unfaithfulness to the covenant is found elsewhere in the psalms. Many of the laments hold God accountable for letting chaos break into the life of the covenant people. In Ps 44:9, 17 the psalmist accuses God of forgetting the terms of the covenant:

> You have cast us off and abased us,
>   and have not gone out with our armies.
> . . .
> All this has come upon us,
>   though we have not forgotten you,
>   or been false to your covenant.

Similarly, Ps 74:20-22 charges God:

> Have regard for your covenant;
>   for the dark places of the land
>   are full of the habitations of violence.
> Let not the downtrodden be put to shame;
>   let the poor and needy praise your name.
> Arise, O God, plead your cause;
>   remember how the impious scoff at you
>   all the day!

It also happens, as in Psalm 78, that the people are charged with disobedience to the covenant and ingratitude, which motivates divine rejection:

> They did not keep God's covenant,
>   but refused to walk according to [God's] law (v. 10).
> . . .
> Their heart was not steadfast toward [God];
>   they were not true to [God's] covenant (v. 37).

In the psalms, the prevailing attitude is that the covenant must be remembered and upheld by both God and the people. Both are responsible for maintaining right relationship with each other. The psalmists bring to their prayers a remembered history of covenant contact with God. They depend on God's being mindful of the covenant for "a thousand generations" of promise to the descendants of Abraham, Isaac, Jacob (Ps 105:8-10, see also vv. 6, 42). For them, relationship with God sustains all life, past, present, and to come.

> The princes of the peoples gather
> as the people of the God of Abraham.
> For the shields of the earth belong to God;
> who is highly exalted! (Ps 47:9).

The psalmists' understanding of the covenant derives from the Exodus story of deliverance from the bondage of slavery in Egypt. Exodus faith taught that God—at God's own initiative—chose to enter into relationship with the people. It is the Exodus God who, remembering the covenant with the ancestors, the families of Abraham and Sarah; Isaac and Rebekah; Jacob, Leah, Rachel, Bilhah, and Zilpah says, "I have seen the affliction of my people who are in Egypt, and have heard their cry because of their taskmasters; I know their sufferings, and I have come down to deliver them out of the hand of the Egyptians, and to bring them up out of that land to a good and broad land, a land flowing with milk and honey" (Exod 3:7-8).

This foundational story of election, deliverance, and covenant with YHWH sustains hope and trust. There is a real confidence in the psalms that God's promise to Moses, "I will be with you" (Exod 3:12), is a promise to all. God is remembered as having seen the needs of those enslaved in Egypt and as having elected to free them from their bondage. God's attentiveness to human need, deliverance of all in enslavement, and extension of hope for the future are the remembered experiences of covenant. Trust in the constancy of covenant is possible because of God's actions and history with the people.

Pieces of the Exodus story appear in prayers like those found in Psalms 78, 80, 81, 105, 106, 114, 135, and 136. As God heard the distress of the ancestors and delivered them from slavery, so God is expected to hear the prayers of the faithful and to effect their deliverance. If God is absent or failing in covenant obligations, then the faithful rightfully summon God to renewed relationship.

Steadfast love and faithfulness are regular characteristics of God in the psalms: "For YHWH is good; [God's] steadfast love endures for ever, and [God's] faithfulness to all generations" (Ps 100:5, see also Pss 117:2, 119:90). It is as if heaven and earth are bound together on account of righteousness and faithfulness: "Faithfulness will spring up from the ground, and righteousness will look down from the sky" (Ps 85:11). Words spoken in complaint about or praise of God's steadfast love and faithfulness establish and maintain the intersection of earth and heaven:

> For your steadfast love was established for ever,
>   your faithfulness is firm as the heavens.
> . . .
> Let the heavens praise your wonders, O YHWH,
>   your faithfulness in the assembly of the holy ones!
> . . .
> Righteousness and justice are the foundation
>   of your throne;
>   steadfast love and faithfulness go before you (Ps 89:2, 5, 14)

God whose "steadfast love is great above the heavens, and whose faithfulness reaches to the clouds" (Ps 108:4; see also Pss 36:5, 57:10) gives refuge to the faithful (Ps 91:4), remembers the house of Israel (Ps 98:3), does not withhold mercy (Ps 40:11, see also 86:15), requites enemies with evil (Ps 54:5), shames those who trample upon the faithful (Ps 57:3), and delivers just and righteous rulings (Ps 119:137).

To this God of faithfulness and righteousness, the psalmist says "Hear my prayer, O YHWH; give ear to my supplications!" (Ps 143:1). Affliction is sometimes understood as a sign of God's faithfulness and righteousness: "I know, O LORD, that Your rulings are just, rightly have You humbled me. May Your steadfast love comfort me in accordance with Your promise to Your servant" (New Jewish Publication Society trans. of Ps 119:75-76).[2] Covenant is consciously elected by the psalmist who prays, "I have chosen the way of faithfulness, I set your ordinances before me" (Ps 119:30). Covenant organizes the day for the psalmist who declares God's steadfast love in the morning and God's faithfulness in the night (Ps 92:2). Covenant is a cause of thanks to the

[2] See *TANAKH: The Holy Scriptures, The New JPS Translation According to the Traditional Hebrew Text* (Philadelphia, 1985).

psalmist who says, "I bow down toward your holy temple and give thanks to your name for your steadfast love and your faithfulness; for you have exalted above everything your name and your word" (Ps 138:2). Covenant makes possible the bitter words: "What profit is there in my death, if I go down to the Pit? Will the dust praise you? Will it tell of your faithfulness?" (Ps 30:9, see also Pss 88:11, 89:49). Covenant causes joy: "I will also praise you with the harp for your faithfulness, O my God; I will sing praises to you with the lyre, O Holy One of Israel" (Ps 71:22). Covenant refocuses priorities: "Not to us, O YHWH, not to us, but to your name give glory, for the sake of your steadfast love and your faithfulness!" (Ps 115:1). God's name itself is a cause of exaltation (Ps 89:24). There is confidence in the psalms that God's steadfast love and faithfulness will never be removed (Ps 89:33).

No God is as faithful as YHWH God of hosts (Ps 89:8). Faithfulness is simply God's way in covenant. It is sung of by the psalmist and proclaimed to all generations (Ps 89:1). Faithfulness is a way that must continually be chosen by those who "walk in faithfulness" on account of God's steadfast love (Ps 26:3). God "does" faithfulness (Ps 33:4) and the psalmists do not hide or conceal this fact (Ps 40:10). God is praised in the assembly on account of the covenant:

> Full of honor and majesty is [God's] work,
> and [God's] righteousness endures for ever.
> [God] has caused [God's] wonderful works to be
> remembered;
> YHWH is gracious and merciful,
> [God] provides food for those who fear [God];
> [God] is ever mindful of [God's] covenant.
> [God] has shown [God's] people the power of [God's]
> works, in giving them the heritage of the nations.
> The works of [God's] hands are faithful and just;
> all [God's] precepts are trustworthy,
> they are established for ever and ever,
> to be performed with faithfulness and uprightness.
> [God] sent redemption to [God's] people;
> [God] has commanded [God's] covenant for ever.
> Holy and terrible is [God's] name! (Ps 111:3-9).

Assurance of being heard, deliverance from bondage, and hope for a future in a land of promise are life-giving metaphors for the prayers of Israel. With God a new future in a promised home-land is available. Fundamental to life itself is trust in the promise that God will accompany and lead the faithful on a journey to a land that they will recognize as home:

> Some wandered in desert wastes,
>   finding no way to a city to dwell in;
> hungry and thirsty,
>   their souls fainted within them.
> Then they cried to YHWH in their trouble,
>   and [God] delivered them from their distress;
> and led them by a straight way,
>   till they reached a city to dwell in (Ps 107:4-7).

Trust in a realizable congruence between creator and creature enables each generation to inherit and shape the essential beliefs that God is with the people, that God sees affliction and wills deliverance, and that God holds out a future of hope appropriate to that generation's own experience.[3] Exodus and covenant are symbols of God's constant availability to covenant members, individually and communally; of liberation from enslavement of any sort; of movement towards a better future; and of departure from a foreign land of enslavement to one's own true home. Election, deliverance, and covenant awaken and sustain trust for believers.

Trust is born of a people's remembered experience of being heard, delivered, and sustained by a power independent of human control and larger than human understanding. In a very illuminating and insightful study of trust, Carolyn Gratton comes to the conclusion that trust is always initiated by the one who is trusted; it is not a sentiment that the one who wants to trust can call forth at will. Trust is a gift, not an act of the will:

> A jolt to my taken-for-granted grasp of what it means to trust
> came simultaneously with my discovery via the method of

[3] In a very helpful article, "Life, Faith, and the Emergence of Tradition," *Tradition and Theology in the Old Testament* (ed. Douglas A. Knight; Philadelphia: Fortress, 1977) 11-30, Walter Harrelson details the core requirements of tradition and shows how tradition is maintained in a process of continuity and change.

qualitative analysis that trusting is not an isolated attitude that can be summoned at will. An "already there" element of reality to which people are or are not present, the initiative for trusting actually comes from beyond the person who trusts—from the trusted reality itself.[4]

Psalms 11, 16, 23, 62, and 121 testify to the belief that God is trustworthy because of God's actions. Each of these prayers manifests a profound sense of communion with a God whose presence, protection, guidance, and provision are sufficient to and larger than human needs. In fact, life is possible because God is "already there" as a life-giving reality. Psalm 11 opens with the confident assertion: "In YHWH I take refuge" (11:1), and affirms the sovereignty of God as one who is in the temple and who sees what happens to humanity (11:4). God tests the righteous, that they—not the wicked—will behold God's face (11:7). Psalm 16 is a prayer to God for safekeeping (16:1) and an affirmation that with God "my heart is glad, and my spirit rejoices; my body also dwells secure" (16:9). God shows the psalmist "the path of life," and in God's presence there is "fulness of joy" (16:11).

Psalm 23 is an extraordinary testimony of security in God's goodness and mercy: "My shepherd is YHWH, I shall not want" (v. 1). Evil has no claim (v. 4), because God prepares a place of security, goodness, and mercy for the psalmist. The psalmist is sure that God, who is gracious and trustworthy, will provide "all the days" of the psalmist's life (v. 6).

Psalm 62 makes it clear that God is the author of deliverance and honor (v. 7). The psalmist is confident that power and steadfast love belong to God who requites us according to our work (vv. 11-12). The psalmist exhorts the people to trust God at all times, to pour out their hearts to God, because God is a refuge for all (v. 8).

Psalm 121, which is a useful prayer for all times of life, asserts that help comes from the maker of heaven and earth who will not allow "the sun to smite by day nor the moon by night" (v. 6). God, the keeper of all life (v. 7), protects those who go out and those who come in forever (v. 8). Relationship with God forever is a perpetual blessing.

---

[4] Carolyn Gratton, *Trusting: Theory and Practice* (New York: Crossroad, 1982) 169.

In a real sense, all prayer is exploration and remembrance of
the trustworthiness of the covenant. Because of God's gifts of election, deliverance, and covenant, God is the trusted other to whom
words of praise and complaint can be addressed. Lived and
remembered experiences of relationship with God allow trust.
Prayer nourishes the mystery that God operates as an energiz-
ing source, center, and goal of the whole world. To pray with
the psalmists is to be caught up in a process of transformation.
Prayer involves surrender and vulnerability to the demands of
the covenant and the process of its maintenance. Prayer involves
sturdy hope and belief in change.

The process of prayer is the process of maintaining traditions
about God, self, community, and the world in ways appropriate
to lived experiences and inherited beliefs. Covenant allows some
prayers to express confident trust that God is dependable. Covenant permits other prayers to claim that God is at fault. All prayers
arise out of confident trust that the God of the covenant is ultimately dependable or at least ultimately accountable. There is a
dynamic interplay in the psalms between creator and creature
regarding the demands and understanding of the covenant.

The psalms model the fact that participation in the process of
engaging with tradition involves continuity and change. Both God
and the one who prays are subject to change in the Book of
Psalms. Covenant makes tradition "not a boundary but an open
road that connects us with the past and point[s] us in the direction of the future."[5] The act of trusting—or of calling trustworthiness into question—establishes contact between God and
humanity that influences the behavior of both. Prayer is dialogue
that is more than a one-way street. Prayer obliges both partners
to remembrance of the past and to action. Prayer obliges God to
faithful, steadfast care of the covenant partners. Prayer obliges
those who pray to increased knowledge and obedience. Those
who pray do not remain the same. As they participate in the covenant process, they grow and change. They are continually making and maintaining tradition in conventional language suitable
to their experiences. The plurality of their experiences of God
results in a plurality of ideas about the God of covenant.

[5] Carolyn Osiek, "The Feminist and the Bible: Hermeneutical Alternatives,"
Feminist Perspectives on Biblical Scholarship, ed. Adela Yarbro Collins (Chico, CA:
Scholars Press, 1985) 94.

Tradition, by definition, is always undergoing modification. As Harrelson says, "Tradition does not remain fixed; it grows."[6] It is surely true that in the psalms expressions about who God is and how God acts, cannot be reduced to an absolute set of propositions. These expressions are subject to conventions conditioned by covenant. Trust, born of a variety of life experiences, permits discovery and proclamation of a rich spectrum of interactive experiences with God. As we shall see in the following chapters, conceptions and names of God, descriptive language for God, and understandings of God's justice in the world are all dramatic illustrations of the variety of covenant experiences, as well as testimonies to the constancy of covenant trust.

The psalms demonstrate that tradition is a continually developing process of dynamic interaction with God. Even though fixed in number, the psalms as a whole are in fact "an open road," which leads to a life-giving stream whose waters we are beckoned to enter and feel on our own naked skin. Prayer calls us to recover an attitude of being naked before God and unashamed of who we really are. In that sense, prayer is a process of new creation. The God who creates life, freedom, and hope by providing experiences that ground trust is known in a plurality of ways. For some, God is immanent. For others, God is transcendent. For yet others, God is mediated through the experiences of life. For all, disclosure of the Holy is partial and incomplete. Yet for all, contact with the God of covenant is believed possible. It is fundamental to the biblical idea of covenant that relationship with God is the only way to life.

---

[6] "Life, Faith, and the Emergence of Tradition," 23.

You who have done great things,
O God, who is like you?
Ps 71:19b

6

Conceptions and Names of God

CONCEPTUAL DIVERSITY: THE HALLMARK

Bruce Vawter makes three observations helpful to the topics we are considering in this chapter and the next. First, "We do not have from the OT a consistent portrait of God as we would expect to have from, let us say, a *Summa* of the Middle Ages or a *Dogmatik* of the twentieth century." Second, "We have no reason to expect any such consistent portrait, that in fact such a consistent portrait would be a certain sign that the OT sin of idolatry has been committed, namely that we have sought to create God according to our own image and likeness." And third, "The challenge which the OT seems to present to us rises less from the inacceptability of its God-construct than it does from the incompatibility of multiple constructs which may be at war with one another."[1]

Vawter helps us understand that language in the Hebrew Bible for God is not consistent, that consistency in creating a single portrayal of God would be a sign of the sin of idolatry, and that the Bible's various ways of talking about God are not always compatible. These insights about God language in the Hebrew Bible

[1] Bruce Vawter, "The God of Hebrew Scriptures," *Biblical Theology Bulletin* 12:1 (January 1982) 3–4.

also characterize the conceptions of God in the psalms. God is portrayed in the psalms in ways that are not always consistent or even compatible with each other. Diversity is the hallmark of conceptions of God in the Book of Psalms.

This is true because descriptions of God in the psalms are reports of particular historical experiences of covenant encounter. "History as event, disclosure of the divine will and a personal relationship"[2] determines the ideas that believers hold about God. Since historical experience is limited, all ideas of the covenant God are only partial and incomplete. Consequently, in the psalms and in all language for God, expressions about who God is and how God works are historically limited revelations.

In the Hebrew Bible, law safeguards God's identity from idolatry by explicitly prohibiting human-made representations or pictorial embodiments of God: "You shall not make for yourself a graven image, or any likeness of anything that is in heaven above, or that is in the water under the earth; you shall not bow down to them or serve them" (Exod 20:4-5). No graphic depiction or human-made image is permitted to give permanence to a particular depiction of YHWH. God is infinite mystery disclosed in finite history and revealed in a plurality of ways. Human limitation in portraying the Holy is undisputable. Vriezen says it this way: "Finitum non capax infiniti"[3]; "The finite is not capable of the infinite."

At issue in the psalms is not the consistency or compatibility of the various conceptions of God, but rather the practice and maintenance of unrestricted belief and trust in a holy, mysterious God who is disclosed in covenant experiences of many kinds. No single human conception or image can possibly limit, define, or fully express God. The consequence of this understanding is that no expression of covenant is judged unacceptable in the psalms. The sole idea that a faithful person cannot hold is that God does not exist. The psalms express the belief that only a fool says, "There is no God" (Pss 14:1 and 53:1). The psalms assume the belief that God is larger than any one psalmist can tell.

Conceptions of God in the psalms are tempered by the recognition that it is beyond human understanding to fully compre-

[2] Th. C. Vriezen, *The Religion of Ancient Israel*, trans. Hubert Hoskins (Philadelphia: The Westminster Press, 1967) 75.
[3] Ibid., 76.

hend God. When the psalmists ask, "Who is like YHWH our God, who is seated on high, who looks far down upon the heavens and the earth?" (Ps 113:5; see Pss 71:19, 89:6), they assume the answer, "No one or no thing is like YHWH our God." God is holy and thus wholly other, completely set apart from that which any one psalmist could tell.

Encounters with the Holy One and participation in the covenant are reported in a host of constructive ways by means of language that makes of God what experience and poetic imagination reveal. So Vawter says, "The Bible, in its record of history and thought, word and wisdom, has given expression to the God idea in many fruitful ways which challenge us to recognize in them not only the Ground of our Being but also our Savior from meaninglessness."[4]

The psalmists conceive of the God to whom they pray in terms of the particularity of their experience and knowledge of the holy. Sometimes the diversity of their ideas of God are at odds with each other. For example, some psalmists describe God as an immanent deity, while others speak of God as a transcendent being. As the following two verses illustrate, one psalmist idealizes closeness to God, while another psalmist conceives of God as remote from even the world of all other gods:

> But for me it is good to be near God;
>   I have made the Lord GOD my refuge,
>   that I may tell of all your works (Ps 73:28).

> For you, O YHWH, are most high over all the earth;
>   you are exalted far above all gods (Ps 97:9).

In addition, God's nearness or distance can be variously interpreted as either a positive or a negative experience in particular psalms. Psalm 22 pleads with God *not* to be far off because trouble is near (vv. 1, 11, 19). So, too, Pss 27:9; 35:22; 38:21; 55:7; 71:12 express real concern that God *not* be far off. God's closeness in psalms like these is judged a positive, protective experience. In other psalms, however, God's closeness is a problem. Psalm 139 asks with some ambivalence, "Where could I get away from your presence?" (139:7b). Psalm 39 says pointedly, "Look away from me, that I may know gladness before I depart and be no more!" (v. 13).

---

[4] Vawter, "The God of Hebrew Scriptures," 6.

Clearly, the rule in the psalms is not conformity to some uniform ideal of who or where God is or even how God acts. The covenant experiences reported in the psalms simply do not yield a homogeneous portrait of God. The diverse conceptions of God in the psalms reflect the perceptions of the particular psalmists. Their ideas of God do not reflect a hierarchy or system of values, in which some understandings of God are more correct, more acceptable, or more sophisticated than others. The psalms testify to a host of beliefs about God and to an attitude of inclusivity that permits those who pray uninhibited and uncensored freedom to express the particularity of their experience of the covenant. Largess of vision and poetic imagination undergird the psalmists' multiple conceptions of God.

God can be described both as one who protects as well as one who forsakes. God is both just and unjust. God is both near and far, accessible and inaccessible. One expression is not judged right and the other wrong. Conflicting understandings are voiced in these canonical prayers as authentic identifications of the covenant God. Differences are allowed to stand with no attempt at uniformity. Consider the contradictory ideas in the following two examples in which God is described in both positive terms and negative terms. God is just and righteous in the first example as opposed to hidden and terrifying in the second:

> Mighty King, lover of justice,
>   you have established equity;
> you have executed justice
>   and righteousness in Jacob (Ps 99:4).
>
> O YHWH, why do you cast me off?
>   Why do you hide your face from me?
> Afflicted and close to death from my youth up,
>   I suffer your terrors; I am helpless'' (Ps 88:14-15).

The Holy One addressed as God or YHWH in the psalms cannot be reduced to *any* single conception. The only theoretical supposition that *all* the psalms support is the absolute that YHWH is YHWH, or God is God. All other generalizations fall dangerously short of the reality of the Holy Mystery to whom the psalmists testify. The psalms dash the caricature of the biblical God as a God of wrath or *a* God of any one thing, even love. They report intense experiences of the covenant with God in poetic language that does not reflect a hierarchy of appropriate or inappropriate ideas of the divine. Conceptions that contradict each other are left unedited side by side. God is what individual and communal, personal and learned experiences disclose.

Of paramount importance is the notion that the covenant God is wholly other, "holy" mystery. God is "holy" (see Pss 22:3; 99:3, 5, 9); God's "name" is "holy" (Pss 30:4; 33:21; 97:12; 103:1; 105:3; 106:47; 111:9; 145:21). God is the "Holy One" of Israel (Pss 71:22; 78:41; 89:18). God dwells in "holy heaven" (Ps 20:6), in a "most holy sanctuary" (Ps 28:2), in a "holy habitation" (Pss 46:4; 68:5), sits on a "holy throne" (Ps 47:8), and looks down from a "holy height" (Ps 102:19). God's "holy arm" gives victory to the faithful (Ps 98:1). God is associated with a "holy place" (Pss 68:17; 74:4; 134:2). God lives on a "holy hill," Zion (see Pss 2:6; 3:4; 15:1; 24:3; 43:3), on a "holy mountain" (Ps 48:1), on a "holy mount" (Ps 87:1). God dwells in a "holy temple" (see Pss 11:4; 65:4; 79:1; 138:2). God's "way" is "holy" (Ps 77:13). God extends a "holy Spirit" to the faithful (Ps 51:11). God leads the faithful to a "holy land" (Ps 78:54), remembers a "holy promise" to Abraham (Ps 105:42), leads the people upon the "holy mountains" (Ps 110:3). God anoints David with "holy oil" (Ps 89:20). Aaron is protected as the "holy one of the LORD" (Ps 106:16). God is feared in the "council of the holy ones" (Ps 89:7). YHWH is worshiped in "holy array" (Pss 29:2; 96:9).

Though there is considerable theological diversity in the understanding of holiness in the psalms, fundamental to any conception of God and covenant is the presumption that God's total otherness frees God to be and to act in ways that cannot be categorized into systematic patterns. In the psalms, holiness has to do with covenant freedom, choices, and ethical behavior. Holiness is dependent upon relationship or connectedness with the divine. A land, a mountain, a place, a person, even oil is "holy" because it is sacred, kept in reserve, or set aside for or by God. God is holy because God is free and independent of human definition. Ludwig Koehler says that God is not only free of all considerations and conditions, but that God is the absolutely free master of the divine will and feelings—even wrath.[5] As holiness frees

---

[5] Ludwig Koehler, *Old Testament Theology*, trans. A. S. Todd (London: Lutterworth Press, 1957) 52.

God from all limitation, so, too, it frees God's people to speak of and to God in unrestricted ways.

As the God of the covenant is by nature holy and free, so also are God's people holy and free. They are free to live in concert with God and the covenant; they are expected to behave in discernibly different ways from those not in covenant. Life's sacredness and holiness cannot be separated from ethical behavior and the covenant. Holiness is revealed in history, in experience, in holy words, and holy events. Holiness bestows life. Holiness is life. Words addressing God are living expressions of the holiness of God and of those bound to God, sustained and set free by the covenant. Words addressing God in the psalms are thus free, unrestricted, and unlimited because of the nature of God and covenant.

NAMES FOR THE DEITY

The Name "YHWH"

In Exod 6:2, God said to Moses, "I am Yahweh. To Abraham, Isaac, and Jacob I appeared as El Shaddai, but I did not make my name Yahweh known to them" (NJB). God's name in the Hebrew Scriptures is YHWH. This name is "explained" in only one biblical text, the story in Exodus 3–4 of God's appearance to Moses in the bush that burned but was not consumed. Calling Moses to stand barefoot on holy ground, God declares divine election of a particular people: "I have seen the affliction of *my* people who are in Egypt, and have heard their cry because of their taskmasters; I know their sufferings, and I have come down to deliver them out of the hand of the Egyptians, and to bring them up out of that land to a good and broad land, a land flowing with milk and honey" (Exod 3:7-8).

Moses said to God, "When I come to the Israelites and say to them 'The God of your ancestors has sent me to you,' and they ask me, 'What is God's name?' what shall I say to them?" And God said to Moses, *"Ehyeh-Asher-Ehyeh."*[6] God continued, "Thus

---

[6] Reading with *TANAKH,* 88.

shall you say to the Israelites, *'Ehyeh* sent me to you.' '' Then God declared further to Moses, ''This shall you speak to the Israelites: 'Yahweh,' the God of your ancestors, the God of Abraham, the God of Isaac, and the God of Jacob, has sent me to you: This shall be my name forever, This my appellation for all eternity'' (Exod 3:13-15).

Election and promised deliverance accompany the revelation that God's name is *Ehyeh*, Yahweh, traditionally read as *'adonay* or LORD, which some translations signal with special small capital letters.[7] YHWH, God's personal name for all eternity, is powerful and holy. All other names for God are secondary to this specially revealed name. Somehow fittingly, the meaning of YHWH, derived from the Hebrew *Ehyeh-Asher-Ehyeh* is uncertain. It is variously translated as ''I am who I am;'' ''I am that I am;'' ''I will be what I will be;'' ''I will be present as I will be present;'' ''I cause to happen what I cause to happen.'' For Exod 3:14, Walter Harrelson suggests, ''I am who I am (and I will say no more),'' adding that ''in Exod 33:19, where Moses wishes to see God's glory, Moses is told that God 'will be gracious to whom [he] will be gracious and will show mercy on whom [he] will show mercy.' ''[8]

Sometime around the third century B.C.E., for reasons that are not fully clear, the name Yahweh ceased being pronounced and the word *'adonay*, Lord, was substituted. Most rabbis later taught that in the period of the Second Temple the Tetragrammaton YHWH was never pronounced except by the high priest on Yom Kippur when the people would prostrate themselves and recite, ''Praise be the name of [God's] glorious kingdom forever and ever.'' Other rabbis, however, made an attempt to have the people use the name YHWH even in their ordinary speech, though their effort failed since other sources indicate that the proper pronunciation of the Tetragrammaton, the four-letter divine name, was kept secret during the Talmudic period.

---

[7] YHWH (LORD or Yahweh) and *'adonay* (lord or master) are different words. The first is God's name; the second is an honorific title for a male. See Pss 8:1 and 97:5 for verses in which both words appear and are signaled in the translations by the words LORD (all capital letters) or Yahweh for YHWH and Lord (only one capital letter) for *'adonay*.

[8] Walter Harrelson, *The Ten Commandments and Human Rights* (Philadelphia: Fortress Press, 1980) 75.

Rabbinical legends taught that the Tetragrammaton was engraved upon the staff of Moses and kept safe in the Ark of the Covenant. Other legends taught that God created the entire universe by means YH, a shortened form of the Tetragrammaton, since the verb YeHi, "let there be," is composed of these two letters.[9] Awe and reverence accompanies the saying, the memory, and the writing of the divine name. Such great reverence for the Tetragrammaton developed that worn out manuscripts containing the word YHWH were stored away in a *genizah* ("a 'chamber' where unusable scriptural texts were hidden instead of being destroyed"[10]).

When vowel points were introduced into the Hebrew text for the first time in the Middle Ages to indicate pronunciation, the vowels of *'adonay* were placed under the consonants YHWH. Christians mistranslated this word as YeHoVaH, which survives as the word Jehovah, an artificial word still used in the King James Version.[11] Adopting the practice of the Masoretes who in the Middle Ages added the vowel points to the Hebrew Bible, many modern translations, including the New Revised Standard Version, the New American Bible, and the New Jewish Publication Society Translation use the special small case capital word LORD to signal the appearance of the name YHWH in the original Hebrew text. The New Jerusalem Bible reads the consonantal Hebrew text as it stands and transliterates the Tetragrammaton as Yahweh.

Koehler rightly says that YHWH is "the true Old Testament divine name, to which all the others are secondary."[12] Yet no translational equivalency for the Tetragrammaton is without its difficulty. Jewish preference is not to pronounce the word YHWH, hence some do not think it appropriate for us to say the name

[9] See Isaac Landman, ed. *The Universal Jewish Encyclopedia* (New York: Ktav Publishing House, Inc., 1969), s.v. "God, Knowledge of," by Simon Cohen.

[10] Martin Noth, *The Old Testament World*, trans. Victor I. Gruhn (Philadelphia: Fortress Press, 1966) 303.

[11] Brown, Driver, Briggs report that "the pronunciation Jehovah was unknown until 1520, when it was introduced by Galatinus; but it was contested by LeMercier, J. Drusius, and L. Capellus, as against grammatical and historical propriety" (*Hebrew and English Lexicon of the Old Testament*, 218).

[12] Koehler, *Old Testament Theology*, 40. He notes that 6,700 times God is called "Yahweh" in the Hebrew Bible, and that this statistic assumes its proper proportion when compared with the 2,500 appearances of the second most frequently used divine designation, the word "God" (41).

Yahweh. To give YHWH the English equivalency of LORD problematically assigns masculine gender to God.

The alternative I have adopted in this book is to designate the Tetragrammaton by its four letters with no vowels as YHWH. This is acceptable in written work, but presents its own difficulty for proclamation. Our problem is how to speak God's name in our language in such a way as to preserve its special quality as a name holy and free.

In a real way, Moses' question is one with which many of us continue to struggle, "When I come to the Israelites and say to them 'The God of your ancestors has sent me to you,' and they ask me, 'What is God's name?' what shall I say to them?" At the burning bush, God reveals that YHWH (Yahweh or LORD) is God's personal name, and in relationship God discloses what the divine name means. What language can best express this mystery? How can we respect each other's religious sensitivities and preserve the holiness of God's revelation?

YHWH, a God known to the ancestors of faith (see Exod 3:16), pledges deliverance and holds out a future of promise. To Moses who is told, "Put off your shoes from your feet, for the place on which you are standing is holy ground" (Exod 3:5), YHWH reveals the paradox of a bush that burns but is not consumed and a name that can be said but never fully comprehended or fully expressed in any human rendering. All expressions of who God is and how God acts can only be partial and incomplete expressions of the divine mystery. The fundamental disclosure to Moses is that YHWH, the God of the covenant, is one who elects to attend to the anguish of people in bondage and to offer them deliverance and hope for the future. YHWH cares. YHWH comes somehow.

Tradition and covenant faith authorize the psalmists to speak to and about experiences with YHWH in poetic, often paradoxical terms. Seemingly contradictory statements are equally true. YHWH, as a designation of the Holy One, is not bound by consistent or logical human-made categories. The diverse ways of conceptualizing YHWH testify to respect and deep appreciation for the mystery regarding God's identity.

YHWH in the Psalms

During the time of the composition and collection of the psalms the personal name YHWH dominated.[13] It was pronounced as part of the text with seemingly no reservation. Written with the four consonants YHWH, which we now refer to as the Tetragrammaton, this holiest of names was most likely pronounced as Yahweh.

The Tetragrammaton YHWH is the most frequently used divine name in the Hebrew Scriptures as a whole as well as in psalms. In the psalms, YHWH, written in the Hebrew text with the consonants YHWH and the vowels of *'adonay*, appears 689 times; a shortened form YaH occurs 43 times; and a third related name composed of the consonants YHWH with the vowels of Elohim, which appears in the RSV translation as an entirely capitalized word "GOD," occurs 6 times (see Pss 68:20; 69:6; 71:16; 73:28; 109:21; 141:8). Thus a total of 738 times divine designations formed of the Tetragrammaton occur in the psalms.[14]

The name YHWH encompasses great diversity for the psalmists. For example, YHWH knows the way of the righteous (Ps 1:6); YHWH sits in the heavens and laughs (Ps 2:4); YHWH is a shield and a sustainer (Ps 3:3, 5); YHWH hears the call of the godly (Ps 4:3); YHWH is refuge of the afflicted (Ps 7:1). YHWH is accused of forgetting the afflicted (Ps 13:1) and of not answering the cry of those who call (Ps 18:41). YHWH is even asked to look away that one psalmist might know gladness (Ps 39:13).

YHWH is a name for which the psalmists give "thanks" (Pss 7:17; 30:4; 54:6; 97:12; 105:1; 106:47; 122:4). They "worship" (Ps 29:2), "praise" (Pss 113:1, 3; 135:1; 148:5; 148:13), "glorify" (Pss 86:9, 12; 105:3), "fear" (Ps 86:11), and "exalt" (Ps 34:3) the name YHWH, which is a "majestic" name (Ps 8:1, 9); a name which "protects" (Ps 20:1); which they "know" (Ps 9:10); "remember"

---

[13] See Appendix A for a listing of the 803 occurrences of Lord/Lord/God in the Book of Psalms as found in the Revised Standard Version and Biblica Hebraica Stuttgartensia.

[14] A related though different name composed of the inflected forms of the word *'adon* occurs 65 times. "Lord" (with only one capital) appears 60 times with reference to the God of Israel; "lord" (all lower case letters in English translations) appears 5 times with reference to a human master or other gods (see Pss 12:4; 45:11; 105:21; 110:1; 136:3).

(Ps 119:55); "fear" (Ps 86:11); "love" (Pss 5:11; 69:36; 119:132); "trust" (Ps 9:10); "call upon" (Pss 99:6; 116:4, 13, 17); "declare" (Ps 102:21); to which they "sing praises" (Pss 18:49; 68:4; 92:1; 135:3); "bless" (Pss 96:2; 103:1; 113:2; 145:21); are "blessed" by (Pss 118:26; 129:8); are "helped" by (Ps 124:8); to which they "give glory" (Pss 96:8; 115:1); "set up banners" (Ps 20:5); and of which they "boast" (Ps 20:7). YHWH is a name the impious people "revile" (Ps 74:18); a name which the nations "fear" (Ps 102:15); a name by which the nations are "cut off" (Ps 118:10, 11, 12). YHWH is a name which those who are shamed "seek" (Ps 83:16). YHWH "alone" is Most High (Ps 83:18). YHWH is an "exalted" name (Ps 148:13) which "endures" (Pss 102:12; 135:13).

It is not possible for us to do more than sample the variety of meaning attached to the Tetragrammaton as it was used in the psalms. It is repeated over and over with an almost kaleidoscopic variety of meaning, with the assumed understanding as expressed in Ps 50:3 that revelation happens because God chooses not to keep silent. YHWH has chosen a particular people (Ps 33:12) and chooses to bring particular people close (Ps 65:4). Revelation begins and continues because of God's initiative.

Familiar for its statement, "This is the day which the Lord has made; let us rejoice and be glad in it" (v. 24), Psalm 118 in only twenty-nine verses, twenty times uses the name YHWH and six times the shortened form YaH. In English translations these words all appear as Lord, but in Hebrew Lord is variously YHWH and YaH. The phrase "the name of the Lord" appears three times in three verses (Ps 118:10, 11, 12), as does the phrase "the right hand of the Lord" (Ps 118:15 [twice], 16). In this one psalm, YHWH is a source of strength, refuge, protection, and as the verses which open and close Psalm 118 repeat, YHWH is good and worthy of thanks (vv. 1, 29). YHWH is this psalmist's strength and song (v. 14), and YHWH is also the one who chastens the psalmist "sorely" (v. 18). Psalm 118 displays great variety in revealing who YHWH is and how YHWH works. References to the mighty warrior YHWH/YaH as deliverer and protector are familiar associations, but the notion that YHWH is the one who chastens the psalmist "sorely" (v. 18) is distinctive to this particular psalm.

In Psalm 18, where YHWH is also the divine warrior who delivers the just from their foes, the Tetragrammaton is used sixteen times in the text of the psalm and four times in the superscription with similar but expanded references. As the following listing of these occurrences demonstrates, attached to YHWH in Psalm 18 are a rich variety of associations including YHWH as the deliverer, strength, rock, fortress, shield, horn of salvation, the one worthy of praise, who hears cries, thunders in the heavens, has breath that blasts from divine nostrils, is the stay of those facing calamity, the one who rewards and recompenses righteousness, the lighter of the petitioner's lamp, the God who proves true for those who seek refuge. This psalmist asks, ''Who is God, but YHWH?'' and declares that enemies are not answered by YHWH whom the psalmist extols as the God who lives and blesses as the rock of salvation.

Ps 18:0   (0 = superscription) To the choirmaster. A Psalm of David the servant of the **LORD (YHWH),** who addressed the words of this song to the **LORD (YHWH)** on the day when the **LORD (YHWH)** delivered him from the hand of all his enemies, and from the hand of Saul. He said:

Ps 18:1   I love you, O **LORD (YHWH),** my strength.

Ps 18:2   The **LORD (YHWH)** is my rock, and my fortress, and my deliverer, my God, my rock, in whom I take refuge, my shield, and the horn of my salvation, my stronghold.

Ps 18:3   I call upon the **LORD (YHWH),** who is worthy to be praised, and I am saved from my enemies.

Ps 18:6   In my distress I called upon the **LORD (YHWH);** to my God I cried for help. From [God's] temple [God] heard my voice, and my cry to [God] reached [God's] ears.

Ps 18:13   The **LORD (YHWH)** also thundered in the heavens, and the Most High uttered [God's] voice, hailstones and coals of fire.

Ps 18:15   Then the channels of the sea were seen, and the foundations of the world were laid bare, at your rebuke, O **LORD (YHWH),** at the blast of the breath of your nostrils.

Ps 18:18   They came upon me in the day of my calamity; but the **LORD (YHWH)** was my stay.

Ps 18:20   The **LORD (YHWH)** rewarded me according to my righteousness; according to the cleanness of my hands [God] recompensed me.

Ps 18:21   For I have kept the ways of the **LORD (YHWH)**, and have not wickedly departed from my God.

Ps 18:24   Therefore the **LORD (YHWH)** has recompensed me according to my righteousness, according to the cleanness of my hands in [God's] sight.

Ps 18:28   Yea, you do light my lamp; the **LORD (YHWH)** my God lightens my darkness.

Ps 18:30   This God—whose way is perfect; the promise of the **LORD (YHWH)** proves true; [God] is a shield for all those who take refuge in [God].

Ps 18:31   For who is God, but the **LORD (YHWH)?** And who is a rock, except our God?

Ps 18:41   They cried for help, but there was none to save, they cried to the **LORD (YHWH),** but [God] did not answer them.

Ps 18:46   The **LORD (YHWH)** lives; and blessed be my rock, and exalted be the God of my salvation.

Ps 18:49   For this I will extol you, O **LORD (YHWH),** among the nations, and sing praises to your name.

Psalm 68 is also helpful in illustrating the range of meanings which the divine name incorporates. YHWH, LORD, occurs two times (vv. 16, 26); YaH occurs two times (vv. 4, 18); Adonay, Lord, is used six times (vv. 11, 17, 19, 20, 22, 32); and GOD, the special form of the Tetragrammaton YHWH with the vowel points of Elohim appears once (v. 20). More regular forms of Elohim, God, listed later in our discussion of the divine name Elohim in the psalms, appear an additional twenty-nine times in this psalm. Thus, in thirty-five verses, the deity is addressed or spoken of some forty times with a variety of names. Verse 20 helpfully illustrates that there is no distinction in Psalm 68 between the salvific power of YHWH, Adonay, and Elohim: "Our God (El) is a God (El) of salvation; and to GOD (YHWH with vowels of Elohim), the Lord (Adonay), belongs escape from death."

Ps 68:4   Sing to God, sing praises to [God's] name; lift up a song to [God] who rides upon the clouds; [God's] name is the **LORD (YaH),** exult before [God]!

Ps 68:11   The **Lord (Adonay)** gives the command; great is the host of those who bore the tidings.

Ps 68:16   Why look you with envy, O many-peaked mountain, at the mount which God desired for [God's] abode, yea, where the **LORD (YHWH)** will dwell for ever?

Ps 68:17   With mighty chariotry, twice ten thousand, thousands upon thousands, the **Lord (Adonay)** came from Sinai into the holy place.

Ps 68:18   You ascended the high mount, leading captives in your train, and receiving gifts among humans, even among the rebellious, that the **LORD (YaH)** God may dwell there.

Ps 68:19   Blessed be the **Lord (Adonay),** who daily bears us up; God is our salvation.

Ps 68:20   Our God is a God of salvation; and to **GOD, (YHWH with vowels of Elohim),** the **Lord (Adonay),** belongs escape from death.

Ps 68:22   The **Lord (Adonay)** said, "I will bring them back from Bashan, I will bring them back from the depths of the sea."

Ps 68:26   "Bless God in the great congregation, the **LORD (YHWH),** O you who are of Israel's fountain!"

Ps 68:32   Sing to God, O kingdoms of the earth; sing praises to the **Lord (Adonay).**

THE NAME "ELOHIM"

"Elohim," a masculine plural noun which is a "summation of all power and all powers,"[15] is sometimes expressed as "gods" (plural) and other times as "a god" or "the God." The singular form of the noun, "El," is a common appellation meaning "God," with reference to the God of Israel or the god of another nation. "El" is used alone, in combinations with other nouns, and with various grammatical inflections. It is not a name exclu-

---

[15] Hans-Joakim Kraus, *Theology of the Psalms,* trans. Keith Crim (Minneapolis: Augsburg Publishing House, 1986) 22.

sive to Israel, but it is the second most frequently used divine name in the Hebrew Bible.

"Elohim" in the Psalms

Elohim/El or some form of these names, translated into English as God or god(s), occur 440 times in the Book of the Psalms, with 428 references to the God of Israel and 12 references to other gods.[16] Most often Elohim, El, and its inflected forms function as a synonym for YHWH. There is no substantive difference in meaning between the divine name YHWH and Elohim. Both are names for the deity. In the case of Elohim, the name can be joined in a genitive relationship to another word in phrases like "God of Israel," "God of Canaan," "God of Abraham," "God of mercy," or the like. YHWH is never so used, but always stands freely, bound by inflection to no other word in the sentence.

Examination of the references to Elohim and its various forms in Psalm 68 illustrates the fact that the same range of meanings attach themselves to this divine name as attached themselves to the name YHWH. As verse 4 says clearly, God's name is YHWH!

Ps 68:1   Let **God (Elohim)** arise, let [God's] enemies be scattered; let those who hate [God] flee before [God]!

Ps 68:2   As smoke is driven away, so drive them away; as wax melts before fire, let the wicked perish before **God (Elohim)**!

Ps 68:3   But let the righteous be joyful; let them exult before **God (Elohim)**; let them be jubilant with joy!

Ps 68:4   Sing to **God (Elohim),** sing praises to [God's] name; lift up a song to [God] who rides upon the clouds; [God's] name is the LORD, exult before [God]!

Ps 68:5   Father of the fatherless and protector of widows is **God (Elohim)** in [God's] holy habitation.

---

[16] See Appendix B for a listing of the 440 occurrences of Eloihim/El or some form of these names in the Book of Psalms as found in the Revised Standard Version and Biblica Hebraica Stuttgartensia.

Ps 68:6 **God (Elohim)** gives the desolate a home to dwell in; [God] leads out the prisoners to prosperity; but the rebellious dwell in a parched land.

Ps 68:7 O **God (Elohim),** when you did go forth before your people, when you did march through the wilderness,

Ps 68:8 the earth quaked, the heavens poured down rain, at the presence of **God (Elohim);** Sinai quaked at the presence of **God (Elohim),** the **God (Elohe)** of Israel.

Ps 68:9 Rain in abundance, O **God (Elohim),** you did shed abroad; you did restore your heritage as it languished;

Ps 68:10 your flock found a dwelling in it; in your goodness, O **God (Elohim),** you did provide for the needy.

Ps 68:16 Why look you with envy, O many-peaked mountain, at the mount which **God (Elohim)** desired for [the divine] abode, yea, where the LORD will dwell for ever?

Ps 68:18 You did ascend the high mount, leading captives in thy train, and receiving gifts among people, even among the rebellious, that the LORD **God (Elohim)** may dwell there.

Ps 68:19 Blessed be the Lord, who daily bears us up; **God (El)** is our salvation.

Ps 68:20 Our **God (El)** is a **God (El)** of salvation; and to **GOD (consonants YHWH with vowels of Elohim),** the Lord, belongs escape from death.

Ps 68:21 But **God (Elohim)** will shatter the heads of [the] enemies, the hairy crown of him who walks in his guilty ways.

Ps 68:24 Your solemn processions are seen, O **God (Elohim),** the processions of my **God (Eli),** my King, into the sanctuary.

Ps 68:26 "Bless **God (Elohim)** in the great congregation, the LORD, O you who are of Israel's fountain!"

Ps 68:28 Summon your might, O **God (Eloheka);** show your strength, O **God (Elohim),** you who have wrought for us.

Ps 68:31 Let bronze be brought from Egypt; let Ethiopia hasten to stretch out its hands to **God (Elohim).**

Ps 68:32   Sing to **God (Elohim),** O kingdoms of the earth; sing praises to the Lord.

Ps 68:34   Ascribe power to **God (Elohim),** whose majesty is over Israel, and [whose] power is in the skies.

Ps 68:35   Terrible is **God (Elohim)** in [the divine] sanctuary, the **God (El)** of Israel, [who] gives power and strength to [covenant] people. Blessed be **God (Elohim)**!

"Elohim" is also a general term for "gods" and is used to name deities other than YHWH as in the statement in Ps 135:5

> For I know that the LORD (YHWH) is great;
> our Lord *('adon)* is greater than all gods (Elohim).

The psalms, like the rest of the Hebrew Bible, admit the existence of other divine beings like those in the Canaanite pantheon. The existence of these gods was not questioned, though they were assigned lower status for Israel than YHWH. They were rivals to whom the psalmists gave no allegiance.

> I say, "You are gods (Elohim),
> sons of the MOST HIGH, all of you;
> nevertheless, like human beings you will die,
> like any prince you will fall" (Ps 82:6-7).

DISTRIBUTION OF THE DOMINANT DIVINE NAMES IN THE PSALMS

Two divine names, "Yahweh" (LORD) and "Elohim" (God), dominate in the psalms. "Elohim" and "Yahweh" both function as proper nouns or names for Israel's deity. Together, or alone, they designate the name of the covenant God. Stuhlmueller indicates that these names, or epithets of direct address, are distributed in the Psalms as follows:[17]

---

[17] Stuhlmueller, *Psalms 1*, 21. Stuhlmueller's table is a helpful illustration of the clustering of the names in the various books. His count of the divine names is different than mine. I suspect this difference results from the fact that tallies depend upon which text is being examined. In Appendix A and Appendix B, I have

		"Yahweh"	"Elohim"
Book I	(Pss 1–41)	272 times	15 times
Book II	(Pss 42–72)	30 times	164 times
Book III	(Pss 73–89)	44 times	43 times
Book IV	(Pss 90–106)	103 times	0 times
Book V	(Pss 107–150)	236 times	7 times

The meaning of these names is explained in the context of their usage. The poetic language of religious metaphor fills in the particularities of these human-divine encounters. "Yahweh" and "Elohim" are names that designate the deity who is known through a variety of human experiences, all of which are understood to be limited and incomplete. These nouns are quite literally in a class of their own. The experiences of encounter with "Yahweh" or "Elohim" in the psalms are described through human analogies, like shepherd or king; through likening God to an inanimate object, like a fortress or a rock; through animal analogies in which psalmists imagine refuge in God like refuge under protective wings; and through transcendent or suprahuman designations in which God is likened to realities that exceed anything known in this world. In the next chapter, we will survey some of these poetic associations through which the psalmists express their experience of YHWH and Elohim.

shown that the name counts differ in the Revised Standard Version and Biblica Hebraica Stuttgartensia. Still further variation is found in other Hebrew manuscripts.

My soul thirsts for God, for the living God.
When shall I come and behold the face of God?

Ps 42:2

7

Poetic Characterizations of YHWH and Elohim

In the psalms, characterizations of YHWH and Elohim are poetic descriptions or meditations on who God is and how God acts. These identifications of God are reflections of various experiences of covenant and as such are charged with a variety of feelings and attitudes about God's identity. As poetic declarations, characterizations of YHWH and Elohim are built of a network of traits and actions that are associated with the divine names. These associations are not programmatic statements in a belief system, rather they are poetic insights about the Holy. If it is true, as Terrien claims, that "poetry takes its origin from emotion recollected in tranquility,"[1] then it is important that characterizations of YHWH Elohim be understood as poetic expressions, for emotion and passion mark the telling of who God is in the psalms.

Divine identifications are most often metaphoric figures of speech in which attributes or characteristics of some known or imagined reality are transferred to the unknown reality named YHWH and Elohim. By means of explicit or implicit comparisons or analogies, speech to and about God gathers up and speaks a set of associations with its own vision. God is revealed in this poetic act. Since no words describing God are absolute or com-

[1] Samuel Terrien, *The Psalms and Their Meaning for Today* (New York: The Bobbs-Merrill Company, Inc., 1952) 153.

plete, and since the only unacceptable belief according to the psalms is that God does not exist, multiple expressions can rightly characterize God.

Metaphorical statements drawing connections between the unknown Holy One and the world of the psalmists bring into focus a range of meanings that create new meanings in their very expression. Because of the particular mixing of characterizations that each psalm employs, the process of transference between known and unknown produces ideas of the Holy unique to almost each psalm. In the particularity of their identifications of the Holy, the psalmists express understandings of God and realities for God that transformatively coalesce in a revelatory fashion.

Sallie McFague helps us understand that "metaphorical thinking constitutes the basis of human thought and language."[2] All concepts about the unknown are formulated in the language of metaphor:

> Most simply, a metaphor is seeing one thing *as* something else, pretending "this" is "that" as a way of saying something about it. Thinking metaphorically means spotting a thread of similarity between two dissimilar objects, events, or whatever, one of which is better known than the other, and using the better-known one as a way of speaking about the lesser known.[3]

Speaking metaphorically about God for the psalmists means "spotting a thread of similarity" between God and some better-known object, person, or thing in their world.

Thomas Merton's insight about conceptions of Christ holds true for conceptions of God in the psalms. Merton says, "Every one of us forms an idea of Christ that is limited and incomplete. It is cut according to our own measure."[4] Such, indeed is the case with all God language, particularly that in the psalms. It is simply a fact that the ideas reflected in the poetic characterizations of YHWH and Elohim in the psalms are cut according to the measure of the psalmists' particular experiences and limited, incomplete conceptions of who God is and how God works in this world. What the psalmists come to know in the speaking of their

---

[2] Sallie McFague, *Metaphorical Theology: Models of God in Religious Language* (Philadelphia: Fortress Press, 1982) 15.

[3] Ibid.

[4] Thomas Merton, *New Seeds of Contemplation* (New York: New Directions Books, 1962) 155.

poem, what the very act of their prayer discloses, is what they tell about God.

In the psalms, metaphoric statements about God or YHWH arise from reality as perceived, explored, and expressed by the particular psalmist. Language shapes and is shaped by the perspective of the speaker. Undergirding the whole enterprise of naming the experience of God in prayer, is belief in a covenant relationship that entitles the psalmists to hope that both they and God can be changed by prayer. Poetic speech serves as a powerful force in the life of the one who prays and all who hear these prayers, including God. Reality is shaped, maintained, and made by the words the psalmists say to God and about God.

Descriptive statements about Elohim and YHWH in the psalms suggests a broad-spirited appreciation and tolerance in the community of a wide spectrum of ideas about the Holy. No metaphoric statement about YHWH Elohim is censored in the Book of Psalms. Even though the ideas expressed about God are often at odds with one another, the community does not suppress their expression. Conflicting understandings of God are recorded, repeated, and seemingly honored by those who pray the psalms.

Characterizations of God in the psalms fall into four categories of comparisons or analogies: transcendent or supra-human likenesses, human likenesses, animal likenesses, and inanimate likenesses. In this chapter, we can but sample the marvelously rich and varied characterizations of YHWH Elohim employed in the psalms. Nonetheless, this sampling should serve to alert us to the enormously wide range of poetic ideas of God voiced in the psalms.

God can be conceived of in transcendent terms that reflect notions about divine reality as independent of or beyond the limits of ordinary experience. Transcendent characterizations of God include designations of God as the divine creator, the giver of life, the one beyond sexuality or graphic representation, the one like nothing known in the world of the psalmist. Testimony to God as a supra-human reality includes statements like, ''O God, who is like you?'' (Ps 71:19), or ''There is none like you among the gods, O YHWH, nor are there any works like yours'' (Ps 86:8). Those who form an idea of Yahweh as ''the God of gods'' (Ps 136:2) or conceive of giving thanks to Yahweh by singing God's praise ''before the gods'' (Ps 138:1) seem to have in mind a model beyond human experience.

Psalm 104 speaks of God as the creator of the cosmos in extravagant images in which God does things no human could be conceived of doing:

> YHWH, my God, how great you are!
> Clothed in majesty and splendor,
> wearing the light as a robe!
> You stretch out the heavens like a tent,
> build your palace on the waters above,
> making the clouds your chariot,
> gliding on the wings of the wind,
> appointing the winds your messengers,
> flames of fire your servants (Ps 104:1b-4).

"Most High" is the dominant supra-human designation of God. Appearing in twenty-two verses, "Most High," *Elyon*, is a descriptive term sometimes used in combination with YHWH as "YHWH, the Most High" (Pss 7:17; 47:2; 97:9); most often used independently as a substitute divine name, "Most High" (Pss 9:2; 18:13; 21:7; 46:4; 50:14; 73:11; 77:10; 78:17; 82:6; 83:18; 87:5; 91:1, 9; 92:1; 106:7; 107:11); and sometimes used in combination with Elohim as "God Most High" (Ps 57:2) or "the Most High God" (Ps 78:35, 56). This title for God, Most High, makes explicit the claim that the covenant God is a God beyond all realities, human or divine.[5] There is no other god like the Most High God. The God of Israel is the supreme God (see Pss 86:8; 95:3; 96:4; 135:5). For psalmists who use this kind of terminology, the divine names YHWH (LORD) and Elohim (God) designate one whose mystery is best preserved and best described in transcendent terms.

Human-like characterizations also serve as a conceptual basis for some psalmists. To the question, "Who is like YHWH our God, who is seated on high, who looks down upon the heavens and the earth?" comes the answer from one psalmist that God is the one "who raises the poor from the dust, and lifts the needy from the ash heap," the one who "gives the barren woman a home, making her the joyous mother of children" (Ps 113:5-9). These activities could have a human author. Sample passages in

---

[5] Hans-Joakim Kraus suggests that the divine designations Most High, King, and Holy belong to the Jerusalem cultic traditions. See his *Theology of the Psalms*, trans. Keith Crim (Minneapolis: Augsburg Publishing House, 1986) 25–29.

which YHWH Elohim is designated by human comparisons or analogies include those which associate God with activities like those of a shepherd, a king, a judge, a mother, or a father.

YHWH or Elohim is likened to a shepherd in only three verses in the psalms. Because this metaphor has assumed such important meaning in Christian contexts, figuring prominently in many hymns and countless stained-glass church windows, many of us invest it with great significance. In the psalms this metaphor appears in the following limited, though comfortingly familiar expressions:

> The Lord is my *shepherd*, I shall not want (Ps 23:1).
>
> O save your people, and bless your heritage;
> be their *shepherd*, and carry them for ever (Ps 28:9).
>
> Give ear, O *Shepherd* of Israel,
> you who lead Joseph like a flock! (Ps 80:1).

YHWH Elohim is compared to a *king* in twenty verses. The conception of God as ruler takes on a variety of meanings in which God is likened to one dwelling in a holy temple (Pss 5:2; 24:7, 9, 10 [twice]; 48:2; 68:24; 84:3), an advocate of justice (Pss 10:16; 99:4), a giver of military victories (Ps 44:4), a cosmic king of all the earth (Pss 29:10; 47:2, 6, 7; 98:6); the creator (Pss 74:12-17; 149:2); a great King above all gods (Ps 95:3); and a God of unsearchable greatness (Ps 145:1-3).

In Chapter 1, we noted that Psalms 29, 47, 93, 96, 97, 98, 99 are a special set of psalms called "enthronement psalms." The formulas "Yahweh reigns," "Yahweh is king," or "God reigns" signal that these psalms are enthronement psalms. It is an interesting fact that not all the enthronement psalms contain the designation of God as "king" (see for example Pss 93, 96, 97) and that some of the psalms which refer to God as "king" do not contain the formula that is the mark of an enthronement psalm. In the following listing of all the references to God as "king" in the psalms, sometimes the suggested setting is an earthly scene and other times a heavenly scene, with the result that God or Yahweh is variously king of the earth or king of the cosmos:

Ps 5:2   Hearken to the sound of my cry, my *King* and my God, for to you do I pray.

Ps 10:16   YHWH is *king* for ever and ever; the nations shall perish from [God's] land.

Ps 24:7   Lift up your heads, O gates! and be lifted up, O ancient doors! that the *King* of glory may come in.

Ps 24:8   Who is the *King* of glory? YHWH, strong and mighty, YHWH, mighty in battle!

Ps 24:9   Lift up your heads, O gates! and be lifted up, O ancient doors! that the *King* of glory may come in.

Ps 24:10   Who is this *King* of glory? YHWH of hosts, [God] is the *King* of glory!

Ps 29:10   YHWH sits enthroned over the flood; YHWH sits enthroned as *king* for ever.

Ps 44:4   You are my *King* and my God, who ordains victories for Jacob.

Ps 47:2   For YHWH, the Most High, is terrible, a great *king* over all the earth.

Ps 47:6   Sing praises to God, sing praises! Sing praises to our *King*, sing praises!

Ps 47:7   For God is the *king* of all the earth; sing praises with a psalm!

Ps 48:2   Beautiful in elevation, is the joy of all the earth, Mount Zion, in the far north, the city of the great *King*.

Ps 68:24   Your solemn processions are seen, O God, the processions of my God, my *King*, into the sanctuary—

Ps 74:12   Yet God my *King* is from of old, working salvation in the midst of the earth.

Ps 84:3   Even the sparrow finds a home, and the swallow a nest for herself, where she may lay her young, at your altars, YHWH of hosts, my *King* and my God.

Ps 95:3   For YHWH is a great God, and a great *King* above all gods.

Ps 98:6   With trumpets and the sound of the horn make a joyful noise before the *King*, YHWH!

Ps 99:4 Mighty *King*, lover of justice, you have established equity; you have executed justice and righteousness in Jacob.

Ps 145:1 I will extol you, my God and *King*, and bless your name for ever and ever.

Ps 149:2 Let Israel be glad in [its] Maker, let the sons of Zion rejoice in their *King!*

Related to the likening of God to a ruler are the fifteen descriptions of God's activities as a judge who decides the fate of groups and individuals. YHWH or Elohim judges the peoples, nations, the other gods in heavenly and earthly scenes in justice and righteousness. Sometimes God comes to defend the accused, sometimes to chastise the accused. But all of the characterizations of God as a judge presume that God is an equitable and fair judge.

Ps 7:8 YHWH *judges* the peoples; *judge* me, YHWH, according to my righteousness and according to the integrity that is in me.

Ps 7:11 God is a righteous *judge*, and a God who has indignation every day.

Ps 50:4 [God] calls to the heavens above and to the earth, that [God] may *judge* [the covenant] people:

Ps 50:6 The heavens declare [God's] righteousness, for God is *judge!*

Ps 67:4 Let the nations be glad and sing for joy, for you *judge* the peoples with equity and guide the nations upon earth.

Ps 75:2 At the set time which I appoint I will *judge* with equity.

Ps 82:1b-2 In the midst of the gods [God] holds *judgment:* ''How long will you judge unjustly and show partiality to the wicked?

Ps 82:8 Arise, O God, *judge* the earth; for to you belong all the nations!

Ps 94:2 Rise up, O *judge* of the earth; render to the proud their deserts!

Ps 96:10 Say among the nations, ''YHWH reigns! Yea, the world is established, it shall never be moved; [God] will *judge* the peoples with equity.''

Ps 96:13   before YHWH, for [God] comes, for [God] comes to *judge* the earth. [God] will *judge* the world with righteousness, and the peoples with truth.

Ps 98:9   before YHWH, for [God] comes to *judge* the earth. [God] will *judge* the world with righteousness, and the peoples with equity.

Ps 119:84   How long must your servant endure? When will you *judge* those who persecute me?

YHWH Elohim is never named mother in the psalms, but maternal descriptions for God do appear, with both negative and positive reference. One text makes it clear that God is *not* like a human mother: "For my father and my mother have forsaken me, but YHWH will take me up" (Ps 27:10). Other psalms use maternal language with more positive reference. Including the text mentioned above, a total of twelve psalm texts explicitly mention "mother." Six texts refer to "mother" in the singular and six texts refer to the singular possessive noun, "mother's." Six of these twelve references explicitly link God's relationship to the psalmist with actions associated with the birthing process or maternal activities (see Pss 22:9, 10; 27:10; 71:6; 131:2; 139:13). Ps 113:9 speaks of God's concern for the barren woman. Pss 35:14; 51:5; and 109:14 are references to a human mother. Pss 50:20 and 69:8 are references to "mother's sons." The following is a listing of all twelve references to mother/mother's in the psalms:

Ps 22:9   Yet you are [the one] who took me from the womb; you did keep me safe upon my *mother's* breasts.

Ps 22:10   Upon you was I cast from my birth, and since my *mother* bore me you have been my God.

Ps 27:10   For my father and my *mother* have forsaken me, but YHWH will take me up.

Ps 35:14   as though I grieved for my friend or my brother; I went about as one who laments his *mother*, bowed down and in mourning.

Ps 50:20   You sit and speak against your brother; you slander your own *mother's* son.

Ps 51:5   Behold, I was brought forth in iniquity, and in sin did my *mother* conceive me.

Ps 69:8   I have become a stranger to my brethren, an alien to my *mother's* sons.

Ps 71:6   Upon you I have leaned from my birth; you are [the one] who took me from my *mother's* womb. My praise is continually of you.

Ps 109:14   May the iniquity of his fathers be remembered before YHWH, and let not the sin of his *mother* be blotted out!

Ps 113:9   [God] gives the barren woman a home, making her the joyous *mother* of children. Praise YHWH!

Ps 131:2   But I have calmed and quieted my soul, like a child quieted at its *mother's* breast; like a child that is quieted is my soul.

Ps 139:13   For you did form my inward parts, you did knit me together in my *mother's* womb.

Phyllis Trible points out that, "Though often neglected in OT theology, the female images [for God] are especially important for an expanding knowledge of ways in which the divine and the human meet."[6] Her discussion of womb imagery adds to our appreciation of the psalmists' understanding of God or Yahweh as mother. Words derived from the Hebrew root *rhm* appear with regularity in the psalms. The noun *rehem,* womb, appears in Pss 22:9; 71:6; 103:13; and 139:13. In these texts description of God is associated with description of a mother. In Ps 131:2, the psalmist is quieted with God as one is quieted at a mother's breast. The implied analogy here imagines God as mother. Other words related to *rehem* (womb) further illustrate the psalmists' poetic connection of God and YHWH with maternal imagery. The plural of *rehem* (womb) is translated variously in English, but the word that appears in the Hebrew in constructions like the following is *rehamim:*

> Bless YHWH, my soul,
>
> . . .
>
> who crowns you with steadfast love and mercy *(rehamim)*
> (Ps 103:4).
>
> [God] ensured that they received compassion *(rehamim),*
> in their treatment by all their captors (NJB) (Ps 106:46).

---

[6] Phyllis Trible, "God, Nature of, in the OT," *The Interpreter's Dictionary of the Bible Supplement* (Nashville, TN: Abingdon, 1976) 368.

The adjective *rahum* (merciful or compassionate) illustrates a fundamental characteristic of the covenant God. The following examples show that implied maternal analogies for Elohim and YHWH are much more frequent in the psalms than our translations indicate:

> Yet [God] being compassionate *(rahum)*,
> forgave their iniquity, and did not destroy them (Ps 78:38).

> But you, YHWH, are a God
> merciful *(rahum)* and gracious,
> slow to anger and abounding in
> steadfast love and faithfulness (Ps 86:15)

> Merciful *(rahum)* and gracious is YHWH,
> slow to anger and abounding in steadfast love (Ps 103:8).

> Gracious and merciful *(rahum)* is YHWH (Ps 111:4).

> Gracious and merciful *(rahum)* is YHWH
> slow to anger and abounding in steadfast love (Ps 145:8).

God is explicitly named father in the psalms, though the paternal references are far fewer in number than our current linguistic practice would suggest and there is a dissenting voice. Only four psalm texts use father statements to describe relationship with God.

Ps 27:10 says God is not like a father; while Pss 68:5; 89:26; 103:13 claim God is a father. Here in its entirety is the listing of all the references in the Book of Psalms that associate God or YHWH with fatherly language:

Ps 27:10 For my *father* and my mother have forsaken me, but YHWH will take me up.

Ps 68:5 *Father of the fatherless* and protector of widows is God in [God's] holy habitation.

Ps 89:26 He shall cry to me, 'You are my *Father*, my God, and the Rock of my salvation.'

Ps 103:13 As a *father* pities his children, so YHWH pities those who fear [God].

This last text, Ps 103:13, is a special example in which YHWH is named father and described with words that evoke maternal images. The word "pities" or "shows compassion" is *riham*, a word related to the womb word discussed above. God is a father here who is compassionate like a mother. As a father "enwombs" his children, so God is compassionate to those who worship rightly. This beautiful mixed metaphor poetically breaks with the literal designation of God as either an earthly father or an earthly mother to articulate a new conception of the mystery of God. This particular word, *kerahem*, is used only here in the entire Hebrew Bible.

Animal comparisons or analogies for God are also employed, though with less frequency than might be expected. While God is likened to a *lion* in texts like Jer 49:19; 50:44; Hos 5:14; 11:10; 13:7-8; Amos 3:4 and 3:8, in the psalms only enemies are described with lion metaphors (Pss 7:2; 10:9; 17:12 (twice); 22:13, 21; 91:13 (twice). While God is likened to a *bear* in texts like Hos 13:8 and Lam 3:10, there is no similar reference to anyone or anything in the psalms. Nothing in the psalms is like Lam 3:10-11, which describes distress inflicted by God with powerful animal metaphors:

> [God] is to me like a bear lying in wait,
>   like a lion in hiding;
> [God] led me off my way and tore me to pieces;
> [God] has made me desolate.

In the psalms, animal imagery for God is reminiscent of the protective concepts evoked by the *eagle's wings* passages in Exod 19:4 and Deut 32:11, or the reward Boaz prays for Ruth whom he says has taken refuge under the *wings* of the God of Israel (Ruth 2:12). The only animal metaphors in the psalms are six positive protective references to God that refer to the shadow or the shelter or God's *wings*:

> Keep me as the apple of the eye;
>   hide me in the *shadow of your wings*,
> from the wicked who despoil me,
>   my deadly enemies who surround me (Ps 17:8-9).

> How precious is your steadfast love, O God!
>   The children of humankind take refuge
>   *in the shadow of your wings* (Ps 36:7).

Be merciful to me, O God, be merciful to me,
   for in you I take refuge;
in the shadow of your wings I take refuge,
   until the destruction is past (Ps 57:1).

Let me dwell in your tent for ever!
   Oh to be safe *under the shelter of your wings!* (Ps 61:4).

For you have been my help,
   and under *the shadow of your wings* I sing for joy (Ps 63:7).

[God] will cover you with [God's] pinions,
   and *under* [God's] *wings* you will find refuge (Ps 91:4).

Inanimate analogies for God and Yahweh are regularly employed. God is a fortress, a rock, a shield, water, light. For the sake of a sense of these terms, consider the texts which designate God as a "rock." Notice that the terms are not literal correlations. God is not in any sense literally a rock, any more than God is literally a bird, shepherd, judge, father, mother, or king. The God of the covenant is a God of mystery, a God known in the paradox of a bush that does not burn and a name, YHWH, that cannot be translated.

Ps 18:2   YHWH is my **rock,** and my fortress, and my deliverer, my God, my **rock,** in whom I take refuge, my shield, and the horn of my salvation, my stronghold.

Ps 18:31   For who is God, but YHWH? And who is a **rock,** except our God?—

Ps 18:46   YHWH lives; and blessed be my **rock,** and exalted be the God of my salvation,

Ps 19:14   Let the words of my mouth and the meditation of my heart be acceptable in your sight, YHWH, my **rock** and my redeemer.

Ps 28:1   To you, YHWH, I call; my **rock,** be not deaf to me, lest, if you be silent to me, I become like those who go down to the Pit.

Ps 31:2   Incline your ear to me, rescue me speedily! Be a **rock** of refuge for me, a strong fortress to save me!

Ps 31:3   Yea, you are my **rock** and my fortress; for your name's sake lead me and guide me,

Ps 42:9　I say to God, my **rock:** "Why have you forgotten me? Why go I mourning because of the oppression of the enemy?"

Ps 62:2　[God] only is my **rock** and my salvation, my fortress; I shall not be greatly moved.

Ps 62:6　[God] only is my **rock** and my salvation, my fortress; I shall not be shaken.

Ps 62:7　On God rests my deliverance and my honor; my mighty **rock,** my refuge is God.

Ps 71:3　Be to me a **rock** of refuge, a strong fortress, to save me, for you are my **rock** and my fortress.

Ps 78:35　They remembered that God was their **rock,** the Most High God their redeemer.

Ps 89:26　He shall cry to me, 'You are my Father, my God, and the **Rock** of my salvation.'

Ps 92:15　to show that YHWH is upright; [God] is my **rock,** and there is no unrighteousness in [God].

Ps 94:22　But YHWH has become my stronghold, and my God the **rock** of my refuge.

Ps 95:1　O come, let us sing to YHWH; let us make a joyful noise to the **rock** of our salvation!

Ps 144:1　Blessed be YHWH, my **rock,** who trains my hands for war, and my fingers for battle;

Ps 144:2　my **rock** and my fortress, my stronghold and my deliverer, my shield and [the one] in whom I take refuge, who subdues the peoples.

In the psalms, characterizations of God function to bring into focus a range of identifications that create new identifications in their very expression. Mixed metaphors preserve the mystery of God and at the same time reveal who God is and how God acts. Brueggemann helpfully says of the psalms that their language "is not only for candor but for the articulation of that which is known both by God and by human persons only when articulated. That is everything depends on the articulation, for such speech evokes something quite new for both parties in the conversation."[7] Revelation is born in the finding of a voice to tell who God is and how God acts.

[7] Walter Brueggemann, *Praying the Psalms* (Winona, MN: Saint Mary's Press, 1984) 11.

God is truly good to the upright,
to those whose heart is pure.
Ps 73:1

8

Understandings of God's Justice

THEODICY AND THE PRACTICE OF FAITH

The issue of God and justice (theodicy: Θεός, *God* and δίκη, *justice*) is a question for people of faith in good times as well as in bad. What does it mean that the righteous suffer and the wicked prosper? Why do innocent children suffer illness and death? What does it mean that anyone prospers at all? How does covenant with God work in this world?

Brueggemann says, "If spirituality is a concern for *communion with God*, theodicy is concern for a *fair deal*."[1] In all seasons of life, the faithful are concerned with a "fair deal" from God. In good times, when relationship with God is comfortable, it is easy to assume things are right with God, selves, and others. In such times, it seems that "God is truly good to the upright, to those whose heart is pure" (Ps 73:1).

In bad times, when bad things happen, some question God, selves, and others. When relationship with God is not comfortable, the faithful may ask whether they are getting a "fair deal" or not? Jeremiah poses this issue sharply:

> You will be in the right, O Lord, if I make a claim against You,
> Yet I shall present charges against You:

---

[1] Brueggemann, *The Message of the Psalms*, 169.

Why does the way of the wicked prosper?
Why are the workers of treachery at ease?

(Jer 12:1, New JPS Trans.)

The beliefs, attitudes, and practice of prayer in the Book of Psalms suggest that the psalmists never found one fully satisfying response or solution to the difficult problem of reconciling God's identity and actions with life experiences of evil. In fact, nowhere in the Hebrew Scriptures is the tension between belief in a benevolent, providential covenant God and the experience of evil which causes suffering finally resolved in a way that testifies to a single answer that emerges as the solution for this very difficult problem. In the psalms, as in the rest of the Hebrew Scriptures, there are at least seven alternative solutions to the issue of theodicy that suggest ways of understanding, interpreting, and bearing suffering and the existence of evil.

The alternative solutions to the problem of theodicy grow out of an understanding of covenant that incorporates the belief that in relationship with God suffering is a bearable part of life. Covenant with God mitigates suffering in that the sufferer is never alone, but covenant is not an exemption from suffering or a guarantee that evil will not touch the covenant partner. The psalms reflect an appreciation of the covenant as a dynamic process in which suffering and evil can find a place. Covenant faithfulness, as expressed in the prayers of the psalmists, testifies to multiple ways of coping with suffering. Humans are responsible as created beings and God is responsible as creator of both good and evil in the world to deal "fairly" with one another.

ALTERNATIVE OLD TESTAMENT SOLUTIONS[2]

1. *Human sinfulness* is the most common explanation of the existence of suffering. In this view, disruption of life's harmony is understood as a result of distorted human choices. Restoration comes from God's forgiveness. A psalmist with such an attitude prays:

[2] James Crenshaw, "Theodicy," *The Interpreter's Dictionary of the Bible Supplement* (Nashville, TN: Abingdon, 1976) 895–896, lists six of the seven alternative solutions to the problem of theodicy employed in this chapter.

> Have mercy on me, O God, according
> to your steadfast love;
> according to your abundant mercy
> blot out my transgressions,
> Wash me thoroughly from my iniquity,
> and cleanse me from my sin! (Ps 51:1-2).

In this interpretation, God acts primarily as an impartial judge who punishes evil and rewards good, rendering to all according to their deeds (see also Pss 28:4; 62:12). This sentiment is expressed by the psalmist who says, "YHWH preserves the faithful, but abundantly requites the one who acts haughtily" (Ps 31:23).

Bad things happen as a result of bad human choices made either by self or others. Some psalms indict the one who prays as the source of the difficulty. The following citations exemplify the understanding that human sinfulness is the cause of suffering. The following translations are all taken from *The New Jerusalem Bible:*

> I said not a word, but my bones wasted away
>   from groaning all the day;
> day and night
>   your hand lay heavy upon me;
> my heart grew parched as stubble
>   in summer drought.
> I made my sin known to you,
>   did not conceal my guilt.
> I said, "I shall confess
>   my offense to Yahweh."
> And you, for your part, took away my guilt,
>   forgave my sin (Ps 32:3-5).

> Your indignation has left no part of me unscathed,
> my sin has left no health in my bones.
> My sins stand higher than my head,
> they weigh on me as unbearable weight.
> I have stinking, festering wounds,
> thanks to my folly.
> I am twisted and bent double,
> I spend my days in gloom.
> My loins burn with fever,
> no part of me is unscathed.

Numbered and utterly crushed
I groan in distress of heart (Ps 38:3-8).

Have mercy on me, O God, in your faithful love,
in your great tenderness wipe away my offences;
wash me thoroughly from my sin.
For I am well aware of my offences,
my sin is constantly in mind.
Against you, you alone, I have sinned,
I have done what you see to be wrong,
that you may show your saving justice when you pass sentence,
and your victory may appear when you give judgment
(Ps 51:1-4).

If you kept record of our sins,
   Lord, who could stand their ground?
But with you is forgiveness,
   that you may be revered (Ps 130:3-4).

Though some of the psalmists admit human sinfulness as a cause of suffering, more often another is imputed as the party responsible for causing suffering. "Enemies," often called "evildoers" or "workers of evil," are responsible for the evil that befalls the one who prays (see Pss 6:8; 28:3; 53:4; 59:2; 64:1-6; 94:3-7, 16; 125:5; 141:4, 9).[3] God is expected to deal fairly by punishing these wicked others for their deeds.

While the most common explanation of suffering is human sinfulness, this solution did not go unchallenged in the Old Testament and it surely does not dominate in the psalms.[4] The Book of Job thoroughly attacks the theology proposed by the Deuteronomistic authors who taught: "If you obey the voice of YHWH your God, being careful to do all the commandments which I command you this day, YHWH your God will set you high above all the nations of the earth. And all these blessings shall come upon you and overtake you, if you obey the voice of YHWH your God" (Deut 28:1-2). Job was an obedient servant,

---

[3] For additional information on enemies and evildoers, see Leopold Sabourin, *The Psalms: Their Origin and Meaning* (New York: Alba House, 1974) 115–117. See also "The Enemy Powers" in Hans-Joakim Kraus, *Theology of the Psalms*, trans. Keith Crim (Minneapolis, MN: Augsburg Publishing House, 1986) 125–136.

[4] Most psalms judge suffering as caused by something external to or outside the psalmist, most often either an enemy or God.

but Job was neither blessed nor treated fairly by God or his friends. The authors of the Book of Job take sharp issue with too simple and universal an explanation of suffering.[5] The psalms, too, testify to more than one reason for human suffering.

2. *Suffering as a divine pedagogical tool* is another biblical solution to the existence of evil. God chastises nations or individuals in order to teach righteousness and justice (Pss 94:10; 118:18). Happy is the one whom God chastens and teaches by dire adversity (Ps 94:12; Job 5:17). The divine words, which might have been spoken by a priest or temple servant in a liturgical context, in Ps 32:6-8 make it clear that in a time of stress the godly should confess sin and offer prayer to God. Protection and deliverance are available to the one who hears God's counsel: "I will instruct you and teach you the way you should go; I will counsel you with my eye upon you" (Ps 32:8).

Suffering, then, is sometimes understood as one of God's ways of provoking a teachable moment in which the faithful can learn the way to right relationship with God, self, and community. Chastisement is a sign of God's enduring love from which the one corrected and the community receive instruction about God's ways.

Suffering leads to God for those who espouse this orientation. However, this view, too, is challenged by the psalms themselves. Some psalmists want to avoid divine chastisement as a way to God. Two psalmists specifically pray, "YHWH, Rebuke me not in your anger, nor chasten me in your wrath" (Pss 6:1 and 38:1).

Many psalms idealize God as a teacher with no mention of suffering (see, for instance, Pss 25:4; 25:5; 27:11; 51:6; 86:11; 90:12). Classic positive attitudes to God as teacher are expressed in Psalm 119:12, 26, 29, 33, 64, 66, 68, 108, 124, 135, 171 in which the psalmist prays for gracious instruction in God's ways and statutes. Since rebuke is reserved for those who wander from God's ways (Ps 119:21), it may be that this psalm supports the idea of correction as a divine pedagogical tool.

Clearly the psalms champion the sentiment that, no matter what the cost, it is right to pray: "Lead me in your truth, and teach me, for you are the God of my salvation" (Ps 25:4).

---

[5] Roland Murphy says that the traditional view of retribution is shown to be inadequate in Job. "It has its truth, but neither can it be pressed. It comes to shipwreck on Job's case" (*The Psalms, Job,* 81; see also 61–62).

3. *Theophany*, a manifestation of God's presence in human life, is a third resolution of theodicy. Delight in God's presence renders struggle with evil unnecessary. Suffering and the existence of evil do not matter when God is recognized. Those upon whom God's face shines are safe (Ps 80:3, 7, 19), untroubled, and even joyful, despite suffering.

> As for me, I shall behold your face
> in righteousness;
> when I awake, I shall be satisfied
> with beholding your form (Ps 17:15).

With theophany, questions of equity or guilt give way to the power of communion. The one who suffers is "caught up" or "received" *(laqah)* by God. With confidence, the psalmist can pray, "God will ransom my soul from the power of Sheol, God will *catch me up*" (Ps 49:15).

"Psalm 73 boldly expresses the highest assurance, that out of sorrow and suffering God's servant will be caught up into 'glory,' into the splendor of the realm of God."[6] This psalm opens with the foundational assertion that "God is truly good to the upright, to those whose heart is pure" (Ps 73:1). As the psalm develops, it puts to test this assertion. First the psalmist faces responsibility for "almost stumbling" (Ps 73:2), acknowledging jealousy over the prosperity of the wicked (vv. 3-12). Then the poet goes "into the sanctuary of God" (v. 17) and life takes on a new look:

> My mind was stripped of its reason,
> my feelings were numbed.
> I was a dolt, without knowledge;
> I was brutish toward You.
> Yet I was always with You,
> You held my right hand;
> You guided me by Your counsel
> and afterward *receive (laqah)* me with glory.
> Whom else have I in heaven?
> And having You, I want no one on earth.
> My body and mind fail;
> but God is the stay of my mind, my portion forever.

[6] Hans-Joachim Kraus, *Theology of the Psalms*, 174.

> Those who keep far from You perish;
>   You annihilate all who are untrue to You.
> As for me, nearness to God is good;
> I have made the Lord God my refuge,
>   that I may recount all Your works (Ps 73:21-28).[7]

Resolution to suffering, actually dissolution of the problem, comes from the joy of communion with God. When one who suffers is caught up by God, questions about suffering disappear.

4. *An eschatological response* is also found in the Hebrew Scriptures and the psalms. In a time to come God will rectify injustice. God-Who-Comes will judge the wicked, save the righteous, and make equity accessible. When God's reign is realized, the heavens and the earth shall rejoice, for God will come to judge the earth and the world with righteousness and the people with truth:

> Let the heavens be glad, and let the earth rejoice;
>   let the sea roar, and all that fills it;
>   let the field exult, and everything in it!
> Then shall all the trees of the wood sing for joy
>   before YHWH, who comes,
>   who comes to judge the earth.
> YHWH will judge the world with righteousness,
>   and the peoples with truth (Ps 96:11-13).

Eschatological hope is hope in a near future, hope based on the experience of God's past acts of deliverance (see Pss 47, 97, 98, 99). Joy, justice, and judgment will be accomplished in God's time, a time expected now and at the end of the world. It is significant that most of the Old Testament has little to say about life beyond the grave as a means of deliverance from suffering.[8] In the Hebrew Bible eschatology is a this–worldly hope that understands the future to be completely in the hands of God. Such hope requires that the faithful "serve YHWH with fear and trembling" (Ps 2:11) for righteousness, victory, and dominion belong to God.

---

[7] New Jewish Publication Society translation, reading with the note for v. 24b, emphasis and Hebrew added.

[8] All the dead descended to Sheol, a place where there was no praise or remembrance of God (Pss 6:5; 28:1; 30:9). Sheol was a "land of silence" (Ps 94:17; see also Ps 115:17). Nowhere in the Old Testament is Sheol regarded as a place of punishment. The concept of "hell" as a place of damnation first appears in the pseudepigraphic Book of Enoch, likely composed in the first century B.C.E.

5. *God is unjust* is a radical biblical response to the existence of evil. In this view, God's actions are accounted for as the result of God's freedom to act as God wills. God is responsible for the distress of the one who is troubled.

> I am reckoned among those who go down to the Pit;
>   I am a person who has no strength,
> like one forsaken among the dead,
>   like the slain that lie in the grave,
> like those whom you remember no more,
>   for they are cut off from your hand.
> *You* have put me in the depths of the Pit,
>   in the regions dark and deep.
> *Your* wrath lies heavy upon me,
>   and *you* overwhelm me with all your waves (Ps 88:4-7, emphasis added).

In this understanding of suffering, God is at fault. God is accused of being unfaithful to the covenant. In Psalm 44, which is a national lament after defeat in battle, the people and king recount their confidence in God's past dealing with their ancestors. Not in bow or sword have they trusted, but in God (Ps 44:4-8). Yet God has cast them off and caused their loss (Ps 44:9-16). They protest, "All this has come upon us, though we have not forgotten you, or been false to your covenant" (Ps 44:17). Because of God, not because of their fault, they are slain (Ps 44:22). They summon God to awake and forget not their affliction. "Rise, come to our help! Deliver us for the sake of your steadfast love!" (Ps 44:26).

This solution to the problem of evil is to put before God the perplexing problem that God has failed to provide defense and deliverance. The resolution is an existential one in which faith propels the sufferers before God with a prayer of accusation that God is at fault (see Ps 44:22) as well as with a prayer of trust that suffering can not be allowed to continue for ever (Ps 44:24). God is summoned to renewed covenant responsibility in this understanding of the existence of evil. In one instance, God is asked "to look away" that the psalmist might know gladness (Ps 39:13). More usual, however, is the confident—if troubled—turning to God in the day of affliction with the expectation of love, promise, graciousness, and compassion (see Ps 77:7-9).

6. *Redemptive suffering* is a response in which one person suffers vicariously for the sake of self and others. An example of this understanding of suffering is posed in Isaiah where the servant is described as one who has "borne our griefs and carried our sorrows," one who was "wounded for our transgressions" and "bruised for our iniquities." Upon this servant "was the chastisement that made us whole" (Isa 53:4-5).

Twice in Exodus 32, Moses intercedes on behalf of the covenant people. Moses begs God not to consume the people (Exod 32:11-13). Moses admits to God, "This people have sinned a great sin; they have made for themselves gods of gold. But now, if you will forgive their sin—and if not, blot me, I pray you, out of your book which you have written" (Exod 32:31-32).

The concept of taking upon self the fault of others appears in Psalm 106 where it is stated that God would have destroyed the people had not Moses, God's chosen one, "stood in the breach" before God to avert God's wrath and destruction (Ps 106:23; compare Exod 32).

More usually in the psalms, redemptive suffering is alluded to indirectly. "Let this be recorded for a generation to come, so that a people yet unborn may praise YHWH" (Ps 102:18) serves as an example of a lament prayed for both self and others yet to come. And the psalmist who invites worshipers in Zion to consider well the towers, ramparts, and citadels of Zion so that they might "tell the next generation that this is God" (Ps 48:13) illustrates an orientation to faith that includes the belief that what happens to one happens to others in the community.

The psalms illustrate the inescapable relatedness of suffering and life. Finally, they refuse to resolve why suffering that results from evil exists in the world. No one way of understanding this difficult issue is judged better than the others outlined above. We have much to learn from all of the alternatives proposed in the psalms. Surely, we cannot hastily adopt one particular way of praying about suffering and remain true to the message of the psalms. There is great variety and richness of response to this complex issue in Israel's prayers. Various psalmists respond faithfully to suffering in various ways.

The psalms make it clear that there are diverse faithful responses to suffering. Knowledge of these diverse responses allows those who suffer access to wisdom. Our task in studying and praying the psalms is to grow in wisdom and in understanding of what it means to maintain tradition by engaging in dynamic relationship with God. Relationship with God—whatever shape that takes for an individual or a community—is finally what counts most. In faith, we believe that God is always with us, that the covenant is reliable and life-giving.

To that end, then, a seventh word about theodicy, the question of God's existence and justice.

7. *Presumption of God's justice* is a widespread assumption. Much of the time the psalmists do not worry about why evil and suffering exist. This does not mean that theodicy is not an issue, it simply means that the issue does not surface. God is unquestionably understood as just, good, benevolent:

> YHWH lives; and blessed be my rock,
>   and exalted be the God of my salvation (Ps 18:46).
>
> Though I walk in the midst of trouble,
>   you preserve my life;
> you stretch out your hand against the
>   wrath of my enemies (Ps 138:7).

In times of well-being and equilibrium, the faithful unquestioningly believe in God's promise to love, deliver, protect, rescue (see Ps 91:14-16). Conventional piety is not, however, narrowly or restrictively absolutized as the only way of faithful response. The genius of the spirituality of the psalms is that the preponderance of laments stand as witness that the faithful include people troubled by suffering. The practice of prayer as described in the psalms assumes a plurality of modes of access to the God of the covenant. God stands with all—the troubled and the untroubled alike, ready to deliver, and to hold out hope for the future.

In good times as well as in bad, God is God. No matter what conception of God or what language describes God, God is present as a covenant partner. Tradition teaches that conventional practices permit variety. Faith requires relationship with God. In all times, the psalmists model the choice of a way of response that leads to increasing congruence with God and the vision God discloses to them individually and communally. Prayer is a vehicle for increased congruity. The admonition of Psalm 37 "fret not yourself because of the wicked" (vv. 1, 7, 8) turns out to be true in good times as well as bad.

Indeed, there is finally no need "to fear in times of trouble" (Ps 49:5). Covenant provides no easy answer, but it does claim that there is a way to survive because God and relationship with God are available to all. There is no need to deny the existence of evil. There is also no need to defend God. Consensus is not necessary in the psalms. God and God's justice (theodicy) are real, inescapable issues for all who pray. In at least seven ways, the psalms say that life and suffering exist together.

Evil, however, does not get the last word. The psalms illustrate that evil finds a place in the lives of those who are in covenant with the God of Israel. In a variety of ways, covenant with God brings life and hope for a future, even while the features of this future are as yet undisclosed.

> The question 'Why do the innocent suffer?' is transformed into 'How does history work?' The answer that Israel knew very well is that history works through social processes. . . . Those social processes are either legitimated or judged by God. They operate either equitably or unjustly, either for the well-being of the community or for its destruction. That is how history works. Yahweh is discerned in Israel, sometimes as the *impetus of the social process*, sometimes as the norm, and sometimes as the *agent for the transformation* of the process.[9]

[9] Walter Brueggemann, "Theodicy in a Social Dimension," *Journal for the Study of the Old Testament* 33 (1985) 21.

III. PRAYER AS A VEHICLE FOR UNDERSTANDING GOD AND SELF

"Noverim te, noverim me."
"May I know you, may I know myself!"
St. Augustine

9

Wholeheartedness in Prayer

The commandment, "Thou shalt not make unto thee an image," means at the same time, "Thou canst not make an image." This does not, of course, refer merely to sculptured or painted images, but to our fantasy, to all the power of our imagination as well. But man is forced time and again to make images, and forced to destroy them when he realizes that he has not succeeded.

The images topple, but the voice is never silenced. . . . The voice speaks in the guise of everything that happens, in the guise of all world events; it speaks to the men of all generations, makes demands upon them, and summons them to accept their responsibility. . . . It is of the utmost importance not to lose one's openness. But to be open means not to shut out the voice—call it what you will. It does not matter what you call it. All that matters is that you hear it.[1]

In the psalms, the bottom line is human openness to the voice of God. Prayer is finally a matter of the heart, a matter of wholeness, a matter of holiness. Wholeheartedness in prayer involves attentiveness, decision, choice, emotion, and willingness to see threads of connection between our identity and experience and

[1] Martin Buber, *The Way of Response: Selections from His Writings*, ed. N. N. Glatzer (New York: Schocken Books, 1966) 38.

the identity and way of God. In Hebrew thought, the heart is "the central and unifying organ of personal life."[2] In the psalms the word heart is never used to refer to a physical organ. Usually it means "deepest self" and is equivalent to "spirit" (see Pss 51:10, 17; 143:4) or "mind" (Ps 64:6). Heart is the locus of intellectual thought (Ps 10:6, 11), the seat of meditation (Pss 4:4; 19:14; 49:3). Heart is the decision-making organ of the body. Perverted moral decisions are made in the heart (Ps 10:13). Lies are spoken from a "double heart" (Ps 12:2). Right observance of law begins with an "understanding heart" (Ps 119:34) and a "blameless heart" (Ps 119:80). Life–giving choices are generated by communing with one's own heart (Ps 77:6) as well as with God (Ps 119:11).

The way of prayer modeled in the psalms involves the bringing of one's heart into obedient, faithful congruence with the ways of God in holy time and holy space. Reality is transformed by this orientation between creator and creature. As we have seen, the psalms incorporate many styles of prayer and many conceptions of God. To follow the way of prayer in the psalms is not to learn how to say a particular type of prayer—hymn, lament, or thanksgiving. It is not to learn *the* right name for God—YHWH, Elohim. It is not to define correctly God's nature with transcendent or supra-human analogies, human likenesses, animal likenesses, or likenesses to inanimate realities. The psalms do not teach by way of a fixed script. They teach an orientation to conversation with God, an orientation of openness to hear God's voice in experiences of all kinds. "God does not say: 'This way leads to me and that does not,' rather God says: 'Whatever you do may be a way to me, provided you do it in such a manner that it leads you to me.'"[3]

Thoughtful meditation brings heart and mind together. Truthful acknowledgment of experience, remembrance of the past, refusal to settle for discontinuities in life, listening to one's own heart, and calling out to the heart of God—all these are ways to God. The psalmist does not shy away from facing sorrow or from voicing disappointment with God:

---

[2] R. C. Dentan, "Heart," *The Interpreter's Dictionary of the Bible 2* (Nashville, TN: Abingdon, 1962) 549.

[3] Martin Buber, *The Way of Man According to the Teaching of Hasidism,* (New York: Citadel Press, 1970) 17.

In the day of my trouble I seek the Lord;
in the night my hand is stretched out
without wearying;
my soul refuses to be comforted.
I think of God, and I moan;
I meditate, and my spirit faints.
You keep my eyelids from closing;
I am so troubled that I cannot speak.
I consider the days of old,
and remember the years long ago.
I commune with my heart in the night;
I meditate and search with my spirit (Ps 77:2-6).

The psalmist believes that God vindicates integrity:

Prove me, YHWH, and try me;
test my heart and mind.
For your steadfast love is before my eyes,
and I walk in faithfulness to you (Ps 26:2-3).

Wholeness of heart is idealized in the psalms. The psalmists give thanks to YHWH with a "whole heart" (Pss 9:1; 86:12;111:1; 138:1). Psalm 119 congratulates those who seek God with their "whole hearts" (v. 2) and earnestly prays:

With my whole heart I seek you; do not let me stray
from your commandments (v. 10).

Give me understanding, that I may keep your law and
observe it with my whole heart (v. 34).

The arrogant smear me with lies, but with my whole heart
I keep your precepts (v. 69).

With my whole heart I cry;
answer me, YHWH,
I will keep your statutes (v. 145).

A "whole heart" is one that is not divided. It is not a heart exempt from pain. A rightly oriented heart knows what it means to be "appalled" (Ps 143:4). A heart attuned to God knows how to say: "My heart is smitten like grass, and withered; I forget to eat my bread" (Ps 102:4); "I am poor and needy, and my heart is stricken within me'' (Ps 109:22); ''My heart is in anguish within me, the terrors of death have fallen upon me'' (Ps 55:4); as well as ''Insults have broken my heart, so that I am in despair. I looked for pity, but there was none; and for comforters, but I found none'' (Ps 69:20). With the heart one speaks to God (Ps 27:8) words of pain as well as joy. The heart can be ''glad'' (Pss 16:9; 33:21) and the heart can be ''hot,'' in the sense of angry (Ps 39:3). The heart can ''throb'' with loss of strength (Ps 38:10), and ''overflow with a goodly theme'' (Ps 45:1). Bitterness can be experienced as being ''pricked in the heart'' (Ps 73:21), and joy can fill the heart more than an ''abundance of grain and wine'' (Ps 4:7). Troubles make the heart melt ''like wax'' (Ps 22:14); wine ''gladdens'' and bread ''strengthens'' the human heart (Ps 104:15). ''My heart'' is often a synonym for ''myself'' (Pss 13:5; 16:9; 25:17; 27:3; 73:26; 84:2).

Uprightness of heart matters in the psalms. The psalmists express belief that God ''saves the upright in heart'' (Ps 7:10); that the wicked ''shoot in the dark at the upright of heart'' (Ps 11:2); that the ''upright in heart'' shout for joy (Ps 32:11; cf. Ps 97:11); that God shows ''salvation to the upright of heart'' (Ps 36:10); that the ''upright of heart'' will glory; that God is good to ''the upright'' (Ps 73:1); that the ''upright in heart'' follow justice (Ps 94:15); that the ''company of the upright'' are found in the worshiping congregation (Ps 111:1); that learning righteous ordinances is praising God with an ''upright heart'' (Ps 119:7).

It is in the heart that one waits for God (Ps 27:14), practices courage (Ps 31:24) and steadfastness (Ps 57:7). Trust in God makes the heart glad (Ps 33:21) and enables people to pour out their hearts to God (Ps 62:8).

In the psalms, one disposition of the heart is not better than the other. It simply is. More important than any disposition is the habit of making one's way to God, the habit of believing that prayer changes things. The way of prayer suggested by the psalms is a way with God. The psalmists know that God is with them, or should be with them. They exhort us to ''Wait for YHWH; be strong, and let your heart take courage; yea, wait for YHWH!'' (Ps 27:14). The psalmists do not let their hearts ''turn back'' (Ps 44:18) from God's way. The psalmist prays, ''Teach me your way, YHWH, that I may walk in your truth; unite my heart to fear your name'' (Ps 86:11). Trouble leads one to say to God, ''I will give heed to the way that is blameless. Oh when will you come to me? I will walk with integrity of heart within my house'' (Ps 101:2).

While it is true that elsewhere in the Hebrew Bible the heart is sometimes deceitful and corrupt (Jer 17:9) and inclined to evil (Gen 8:21; Eccl 9:3), in the psalms the godly person is not one who struggles with a fallen or depraved nature. There is a sturdiness of belief that in prayer one can find the way to God, that it is in fact the heart's deepest and most precious impulse and desire. Only one psalm says, ''Create in me a clean heart, O God, and put a new and right spirit within me'' (Ps 51:10). More often the sentiment is that within the heart lies the way, the path of righteousness that leads to God. The psalms speak more often of the righteous who rejoice (Pss 32:11; 64:10; 97:11) and follow justice (Ps 94:15) on account of the disposition of their hearts than they do of fear of an interior evil impulse.

In the psalms, the potential of the human heart is enormous. The way of prayer presumes that the heart recognizes the voice of God when it does not shut out that voice. The right way is known within the heart of the person who approaches God. The implications of the wholeness of heart associated with the way of prayer in the psalms include what is for many of us a radical reorientation. We often think God wants contrition and repentance as prerequisites or consequences of relationship, but in the psalms only once does a text say, ''The sacrifice acceptable to God is a broken spirit; a broken and contrite heart, O God, thou wilt not despise'' (Ps 51:17).

The psalmists express the belief that God will teach the heart to know what it needs:

> Behold, you desire truth in the inward being;
> therefore teach me wisdom in my secret heart (Ps 51:6).

> Teach me you way, YHWH,
> that I may walk in your truth;
> give me an undivided heart to revere your name (Ps 86:11).

> So teach us to count our days
> that we may gain a wise heart (Ps 90:12).

There is no real need in the psalms to get ''fixed'' before setting out on the way. Wholeness is not a prerequisite to prayer. The psalms presume things will be set right in the process of progressing along the way. There is a confidence that God will teach the heart to know, that God will set right the discontinuities of life, be they internal or external. The psalmist is sure, "My mouth shall speak wisdom; the meditation of my heart shall be understanding" (Ps 49:3). The psalmists have simply to go forward along the way, and choose not to turn back once they have set out:

> Our heart has not turned back,
>> nor have our steps departed from your way (Ps 44:18).

> I will study the way that is blameless.
>> When shall I attain it?
> I will walk with integrity of heart within my house.
> I will not set before my eyes anything that is base (Ps 101:2-3a).

> The law of their God is in their hearts;
>> their steps do not slip (Ps 37:31).

Let everything that breathes praise YHWH!
Ps 150:6

10

The Way of an Individual and a Community before God

The way of an individual and a community before God in the Book of Psalms moves into and out of cultic locations, into and out of all the times of life. Claus Westermann says:

> In the Psalms all scenes of daily life are encountered: the house and the road, the field and the workshop, the sickbed and the bedroom; everyday occupations like eating and drinking, sleeping and getting up, working and resting; all ages of life from child to old man and the forms of community: man and woman, parents and children, brother and friends.[1]

Acts of worship in a host of settings order the life of those who pray the psalms. Acts of worship—whether performed individually or communally, within the temple or in another setting—establish and maintain relationship with the Holy One. Acts of worship create and perpetuate the social reality of the community. Ancient Israel understood itself as God's people, a people in partnership with the God of the covenant, a people who yearned for communion with God. Their rich and varied understandings of what it means to praise God, what *tehillim* is all

---

[1] Claus Westermann, *What Does the Old Testament Say About God?*, ed. Friedemann W. Golka (Atlanta: John Knox Press, 1979) 69.

about, challenge reductionistic interpretations of worship in their community.

For Israel "worship" is "serving" YHWH. It is a matter that involves acknowledgment of human and divine dignity. Worship involves belief that the relationship between God, self, and community is of "worth." Quite literally the English word "worship" means "worthship."[2] The words used to translate Israel's understanding of worship are "bow down" or "worship," "serve," and references to the ideal of being the "servant" or "servants" of God. Thirty-seven of the psalms contain some combination of these words, which are forms of the Hebrew *'bd* (עבד) in the verb "to serve" or the noun "servant;" and *shh* (שחה), the verb "to worship," "bow down," "fall down," or "prostrate."[3] The two words עבד ("to serve") and שחה ("to worship" or "to bow down") are used synonymously in the example, "May all kings **fall down** (ישתחוו) before God, all nations **serve** (יעבדוהו) God!" (Ps 72:11).

The attitude in most of the examples is that of humility. God is to be served with "fear and trembling" (Ps 2:11) as well as "gladness" (Ps 100:2). "Posterity shall serve God; future generations will be told about the Lord" (Ps 22:30). The news that God is worth serving is worth telling to God, self, and others.

"All the ends of the earth" (Ps 22:27), the community (Pss 29:2; 95:6; 96:9; 99:5; 102:22; 132:7), and the individual (Ps 5:7) are charged to "worship" God. "All the nations" (Ps 86:9), "all gods" (Ps 97:7), "all the proud of the earth" (Ps:22:29), all the faithful who care about coming into God's presence (Ps 95:6), as well as the one who wishes to give whole-hearted thanks (Ps 138:2) are instructed to "bow down" before YHWH. Psalm 81 admonishes, "There shall be no strange god among you; you shall not bow down to a foreign god" (v. 9).

God's "servant" is idealized as David (Pss 18:50; 78:70; 89:20; 132:10; 144:10), and sometimes specified as a king whom God has renounced (Ps 89:39) and scorned (Ps 89:50). The servant is

---

[2] See G. Henton Davies, "Worship in the OT," *The Interpreter's Dictionary of the Bible 4*, 879.

[3] See Pss 2:11; 5:7; 18:0; 19:11, 13; 22:27, 29, 30; 27:9; 29:2; 31:16; 34:22; 35:27; 36:12; 69:17, 35, 36; 78:70; 79:2, 10; 81:9; 86:2, 4, 9, 16; 89:3, 20, 39, 50; 90:13, 16; 95:6; 96:9; 97:7; 99:5, 9; 100:2; 102:14, 22, 28; 105:6, 25, 26, 42; 109:28; 113:1; 116:16; 119:17, 23, 38, 49, 65, 76, 84, 91, 122, 124, 125, 135, 140, 176; 123:2; 132:7, 10; 134:1; 135:1, 9, 14; 136:22; 138:2; 143:2, 12; 144:10.

elsewhere identified as Abraham (Ps 105:6, 42), Moses (Ps 105:26), and Israel (Ps 136:22). Sometimes the servant is not named but is identified as one formed by the law (Ps 19:11); one who meditates on God's law (Ps 119:23); who prays to be delivered from presumptuous sins (Ps 19:13); who asks not to be turned away by the anger of God (Ps 27:9); one upon whom God's face shines (Pss 31:16; 119:135); one from whom God's face is not hidden (Ps 69:17); one whose welfare God attends to (Ps 35:27); one who trusts God (Ps 86:2); one for whom God's promise is confirmed (Ps 119:38, 76, 140); one who hopes that God will remember God's word (Ps 119:49); one with whom God deals well (Ps 119:65); one whose self is gladdened by God (Pss 86:4; 109:28); one whom God strengthens (Ps 86:16); the son of God's handmaid (Ps 116:16); one with whom God deals bountifully (Ps 119:17); one who dares to ask God how long must a servant endure (Ps 119:84); one whose well-being God assures (Ps 119:122); one with whom God deals steadfastly (Ps 119:124); one whom God does not judge (Ps 143:2); one whose enemies God destroys (Ps 143:12); one to whom God gives understanding (Ps 119:125); and one like a lost sheep (Ps 119:176).

God's "servants" are those whom God redeems (Ps 34:22); those for whom God saves and rebuilds Judah (Ps 69:35); those who hold the stones of Zion dear (Ps 102:14); whose children shall inherit Zion and Judah (Pss 69:36; 102:28); whose bodies were given to the birds by those who sacked Jerusalem (Ps 79:2); whose blood God will avenge (Ps 79:10); who beseech God to return and have pity upon them (Ps 90:13); who pray that God's works will be manifest to them (Ps 90:16); who praise YHWH (Pss 113:1; 135:1); who keep their eyes on the hand of their master (Ps 123:2); who stand by night in the house of YHWH (Ps 134:1); whom God made stronger than their foes (Ps 105:25); those whom YHWH vindicates (Ps 135:14); "for all creation" are God's servants (Ps 119:91).

Worship is serving God and being in "sync" or congruent with God's order for the universe in which God is God and creature is creature. In unison with God, God's servants are partners in imaging God in the world (Gen 1:27). History is the scene of divine revelation and the locus of the continuation of God's covenanted promise to this world. To serve YHWH Elohim is to be freed from all enslavement and servility and freed for worship.

In his discussion of Israel's ordering of time and space for worship at crucial times and places in the life of the individual and the community, Harrelson says:

> Worship is an ordered response to the appearance of the Holy in the life of individuals and groups. Many kinds of ordering occur in the variety of responses that may be called worship, but the gathering at appropriate times and places is of particular importance. It has long been maintained, with justice, that holy time is more important for the Israelite community than holy space. The dynamism of Israel's historically oriented faith makes the seasons for worship more important than the places set aside for such worship.[4]

Life in its totality is divine service. All the psalms are acts of worship that bind both covenant partners to mutual obligations. Covenant is a two-way street in which those who pray do so with the belief that right worship requires attention and self-disclosure. God cares, delivers, and holds out promises in this scheme of life. Prayer is life-changing and life-enhancing dialogue.

Prayer is worship. Prayer orders life. It seems likely that time for prayer matters more than place for prayer, though the unanswered questions about usage of the psalms in ancient Israel's formal worship do not allow us to know with certainty how the psalms might have been used in formal and informal settings. When we call the psalms the "prayerbook of the second temple," we may be skewing our understanding of how prayer functions. Prayer surely functioned in the temple liturgy, but it must just as surely have been part of daily life.

Worship involved cultic festivals, as well as personal prayers, both deriving from a basic attitude of readiness to serve God. Special events in the life of the people included worship in the sanctuary. In the sanctuary at Jerusalem the worshiping community gathered to work out and maintain its identity.[5] It is debatable just how many psalms arose from a cultic origin and how many are personal prayers modeled on older cultic forms. But it is not debatable that Zion, Jerusalem, was the special locus of God's

[4] Walter Harrelson, *From Fertility Cult to Worship* (New York: Anchor Books, 1970) 16.

[5] For a brief summary of psalm scholarship and worship, with an especially helpful evaluation of the strengths and weaknesses of the contributions and influence of Westermann, see Kraus, *Theology of the Psalms*, 73–106.

appearance to the people. YHWH is indeed in the midst of Jerusalem (Ps 46:5). Zion is a "fountain of life" (Ps 36:9). Kraus is correct in saying:

> If we approach the OT Psalms with the question where should one look for and find the God of Israel whom the hymns and songs of thanksgiving glorify, on whom the laments call, and whom all the songs and poems involve, the unanimous, never doubted, and ceaselessly expressed answer is: Yahweh Sebaoth is present in the sanctuary in Jerusalem. Zion is the place of God's presence.[6]

From our preceding study, I should like to add that if we approach the psalms with the question where should one look for and find the God of Israel we cannot overlook what the psalms claim about the heart and serving God. It is a matter of the heart, so to speak, that gets one to the congregation:

> I have not hid your saving help within my heart,
> I have spoken of your faithfulness and your salvation;
> I have not concealed your steadfast love and your
> faithfulness from the great congregation (Ps 40:10).

This same psalm also says:

> Sacrifice and offering you do not desire;
> but you have given me an open ear
> (in Hebrew: ears you have dug for me).
> Burnt offerings and sin offering you have not required.
> Then I said, "Here I am;
> in the scroll of the book it is written of me.
> I delight to do your will, O my God;
> your law is within my heart."
> I have told the glad news of deliverance in the
> great congregation;
> see, I have not restrained my lips,
> as you know, YHWH (Ps 40:6-9).

There is a tension in the psalms that cannot be easily resolved regarding the relationship of prayer in the formalized cult to

---

[6] Kraus, *Psalms 1–59*, 68.

prayer in a personal setting. It is surely an error to describe too readily the prayers as private utterances and an overstatement to subsume the prayers to particular feasts, even the enthronement of YHWH.[7] The question is undoubtedly more complex. It seems likely to me that a good number of the psalms did originate as prayers of the religious establishment, and that an equal or even larger number of the prayers came from outside the establishment from a variety of other settings. Since the psalms mirror the Hebrew Bible in so many ways, it would indeed seem strange if they did not include formal and informal settings for prayer.

If we make an error in reading, I should prefer that we err on the side of reading the psalms as the voices of those choosing to serve God in ordinary life-settings. This perspective grants a voice to the average keeper of covenant, gains least from structure legitimation, and most easily incorporates a prophetic voice. Best of all alternatives to me is recognition of the psalms as prayers incorporating concerns born of both formal and informal settings.

When I consider what we most need to recover from the way of prayer in the Book of Psalms, I think about the inclusivity of the psalms. There is an inclusivity of types of prayer, names and conceptions of God, and ideas about serving God. The psalms model a way of worship that allows for rich variety that far exceeds the narrow way we allow in worship in most of our religious establishments. I see language for God in the psalms like wonderful foods on a richly laden banquet table. Plates are filled high with YHWH, Elohim, and various spicy combinations of these names. Plates are set with names for transcendent imagery, and personal names for God, animal imagery, and inanimate imagery for God. Each guest who worships is allowed to take from this banquet what looks nourishing. Some of this and some of that is likely to be chosen. Metaphors are mixed freely at this banquet table.

When I look at the attitude toward what can be said to God, I also see a rich variety of choices. And all of this leads me to ask, what happened in our use of the psalms to so flatten out the wondrousness of this way of prayer? How did God become

---

[7] Gunkel believed that most of the psalms were private compositions; Mowinckel related most to the cult and presumed a link to a New Year festival. For summary and helpful evaluation, see H. H. Rowley, *Worship in Ancient Israel: Its Forms and Meaning* (London: S.P.C.K., 1974) 176–212.

so exclusively "he" in the language of worship? What happened to the richness of inclusivity in our liturgical banquets? Why do we cling to the notion that there is only one right way to pray? How can we begin to recover an attitude that says both this and that will nourish?

I am encouraged by the possibility that acts of worship in a variety of settings ordered the lives of those who prayed the psalms. Somehow we must each find the way to pull together the threads of our lives and to set our hearts to finding and following the way to God. Communion with God—whatever that may mean—makes life qualitatively different. The psalmists knew that! That truth was written in their hearts.

The way of prayer practiced in the psalms suggests that it is possible for us to express our identity, individually and communally, as a people who believe that God is with us, who hope that God will care about those things which enslave us and deliver us, and who trust that God holds out to us meaningful, good futures. We will need to recover an attitude that there is more than one way to pray, more than one way to name God, and more than one place to establish and maintain intimacy with the Holy.

Brueggemann says, "The lucky ones are not those free of transgression, but those who are able to move beyond it."[8] Movement and choice of direction, these are matters of great significance to those whose way takes them to God.

In the psalms, a plurality of personalities decide life must be lived in relationship with God. Prayers are sparked by focus on God, self, and others. It does not seem to matter that a person prays from a God-centered perspective, a self-referent perspective, or an other-referent perspective. God-centered prayers like Psalm 117, the short hymn motivated by a sensitive appreciation of the steadfast love of God, or Psalm 100, motivated by joyful delight in the thought of belonging to God and serving God are accorded no higher status in the canon than prayers that represent other perspectives.

For instance, Psalm 27, which is the prayer of an individual concerned for personal well-being in the face of enemies all around, says, "YHWH is my light and my salvation; whom shall I fear? YHWH is the stronghold of my life; of whom shall I be afraid?" (v. 1). And Psalm 13, which is also a self-referent prayer, or a

---

[8] Brueggemann, *The Message of the Psalms*, 95.

prayer motivated by concern for self poignantly asks how long God will be hidden and how long will the enemy be exalted. These prayers are not accorded lower or higher status than prayers motivated by concern for others, other-referent prayers, like Psalm 12, a prayer for the poor, or Psalm 71, a prayer motivated by the desire to proclaim God's greatness to all generations to come. What matters is that covenant is so real to the psalmist that no matter what perspective motivates the prayer, it cannot but be given voice.

A voice, a God, experience, the language of poetry—these are the components of prayer. Contact with the Holy—that is the way of an individual and the community before God. Everything that has breath praises God.

The Book of Psalms ends on a high note praising God in the sanctuary with trumpet, lute, harp, timbrel, dance, pipe, and loud clashing cymbals. The final imperative commands, "let everything that breathes praise the LORD!" (Ps 150:6). The way of prayer is the way of life, the way of taking each breath—whether with joy in one's heart or tears in one's eyes—in communion with God.

We who are created of God's very breath (Gen 2:7), praise God with breath. We praise God by voicing our reality. The words we speak to God are good, whether they be hymn of praise or lament. Prayer diffuses all fear save right fear of God. "Worship is holy meeting."[9] In the psalms, encounter with God holds the promise of ordering all life experiences. In this way of prayer, chaos is not destroyed, but it is kept within manageable bounds. In encounter of this sort, the individual and the community are called to find their own voices, to speak boldly to the God who creates new life and new harmony. Faithfulness means speaking to God about matters of the heart.

"In the cult, Israel remembers the holy past, and in the spoken recital it becomes present, for in truth it was meant for every present."[10] Prayer rests on the foundational belief that God can, will, and is now bringing forth and maintaining order. We—male and female—are created in the very image of this God (Gen 1:27). We are made for the work, remembrance, and revelation of this

[9] James Muilenburg, *The Way of Israel: Biblical Faith and Ethics* (New York: Harper & Row, Publishers, 1961) 108.
[10] Ibid., 109.

way of prayer. We speak order into being as we learn to pray with the psalms. James Muilenburg says:

> In the Psalter, we listen to the way of Israel speaking in the presence of the Holy One.
>
> Notable among the features which mark this work of prayer and praise is the large place that is accorded the memorable events of the past. History is drawn into the sphere of the divine holiness. . . . The events are grasped as revelation, and revelation is a call to obedience and service and faithfulness and rejoicing.[11]

[11] Ibid., 110.

Sing to the Lord a new song!
Ps 149:1

11

Reflections on the Beliefs, Attitudes and Practices of Prayer in the Book of Psalms

Many of the psalms talk about singing a "new song" to God.[1] Ps 33:3 says to "sing a new song and play skillfully on the strings, with loud shouts." Ps 40:3 claims that God "has put a new song in my mouth, a song of praise to our God." Ps 96:1 exhorts, "O sing to YHWH a new song; sing to YHWH, all the earth!" Ps 98:1 reiterates, "O sing to YHWH a new song," for marvelous are God's deeds. Ps 144:9 pledges, "I will sing a new song to you, O God; upon a ten-stringed harp I will play to you." And Ps 149:1 delights in festivity: "Hallelujah! Sing to YHWH a new song."

In the spirit of a "new song" suitable for our times, I would like to close our examination of the Book of Psalms with five reflections and a closing word on what I see before us from what is now behind us.

First, a "new song" is born of present experiences. The psalms teach us to pray from lived experiences, whatever they may be.

[1] Carroll Stuhlmueller, *Psalms 1*, 189, explains that the phrase "new song" occurs only in exilic and postexilic hymns where what is "new" may be: "literary, a new role is given to ancient hymns; or pastoral, a new deliverance by God; or ritual, a spontaneous shout or song of the people; or best of all, theological, in that God's redemptive acts are actualized in their full effect within a new generation of Israelites."

Such experiences are by definition ever new and contemporary realities. The psalms are not systematic prescriptions of perfect words to say to God; they are rather models of dynamic prayer that encourage us to pray from the circumstances and in the words suitable to our needs and times. Before us from this study of the spirituality of the Book of Psalms is an invitation to pray wholeheartedly from today's needs in language suitable to our times.

In a book about quite another subject, Marion Woodman, a Jungian analyst, says something about human integration of body and spirit that I believe is consonant with what we have discussed about the psalms:

> Only by opening ourselves to the inner REALITY do we open ourselves to the possibility of the gift of love. Action and ego choice are involved: we can accept; we can reject; we can withdraw at any point. But we cannot make it happen. Love chooses us.[2]

We might paraphrase this as saying that prayer becomes a "new song" when we are open to the gift of love. Most surely, we cannot make a "new song" happen. Only in faith do we believe that a "new song" is our inheritance. Only because we trust that ours is a God who has "put a new song" in our mouths (Ps 40:3) can we hope to sing a song suitable to our experiences and times. The psalms put before us a way of prayer that we can accept or reject or from which we can withdraw at any point. But the fact is that the psalms testify that Love has chosen us not because of what we say or fail to say, but simply because Love has chosen us, where and as we are right now.

Second, a "new song" is a "new" life-melody, a "new" understanding of life's times and places. If "Worship is an ordered response to the appearance of the Holy in the life of individuals and groups,"[3] then the way of prayer is an ordered response to the appearance of the Holy that is ever new and ever old. The way of prayer reorganizes our understanding of the holiness of time and space as belonging to time that is God's time and in space that is God's space.

[2] Marion Woodman, *Addiction to Perfection: The Still Unravished Bride* (Toronto, Canada: Inner City Books, 1982) 188.

[3] Walter Harrelson, *From Fertility Cult to Worship*, 16.

The psalms show that time and space are anchor points for prayer. Relationship with the Holy happens because the Holy has been manifest in a particular time and in a particular place. "This is the day which the LORD has made" (Ps 118:24), whether this day be a good day or a bad day. This is the day when we understand in fresh ways what the psalmist means in saying:

> I was glad when they said to me,
> "Let us go to the house of YHWH!"
> Our feet have been standing
> within your gates, O Jerusalem! (Ps 122:1-2).

Prayer can bring to conscious realization new understanding about what it means to say that our feet need to be within God's gates, that our feet are already within God's gates, and that today and in this place, relationship between God, self, and community needs attention and actualization in prayer.

Third, relationship with God is ritualized in personal and communal prayer. Study of the psalms alerts us to the perspectives we bring individually and communally to forming and articulating language to and about God. The variety of expressions in the Psalter indicates that we need not fear speaking about the covenant reality in language that names our vision, or hermeneutical orientation, of what it means to be fully human and in right relationship with God and the covenant community.

The psalms teach us to value community even as we ponder individually exactly what right communion is and how faithfulness to community, self, and God intersect. Historically it is in community that the bond of relationship between God and people is exercised. In community the divine promise, "I will be with you" (Exod 3:12) finds ritual remembrance and expression. The biblical story works on the premise that it is to members of the covenant community that God reveals the meaning and management of life-experiences.

Dialogue with God—prayer—is both personal and communal. A prophet, like Ezekiel, typifies one called by God to speak so that the community "will know that there has been a prophet among them" (Ezek 2:5; see also Deut 34:10-13; Isa 61:1; Jer 1:2; Amos 3:7). It is for the sake of community that the woman Judith says, "Let us set an example to our neighbors, for their lives depend upon us, and the sanctuary and the temple and the altar rest upon us. In spite of everything let us give thanks to the Lord our God, who is putting us to the test like our ancestors" (Jdt 8:24-25). Prayer does not flatten out individuality or personal responsibility; neither does personal relationship with God take place in isolation. It is to a people that God's revelation is offered. It is to those like Moses, Judith, Ezekiel and the two or three who gather in God's name that the way of revelation is disclosed.

In parts of the biblical story there is hope for a new covenant in a time to come when life's meaning and right management will be disclosed to each individual as God's word written in each one's heart. Such a time of radical reformation and new covenant is described by Ezekiel (see also Jer 31:31-34):

> A new heart I will give you, and a new spirit I will put within you; and I will take out of your bodies the heart of stone and give you a heart of flesh. I will put my spirit within you, and cause you to walk in my statutes and be careful to observe my ordinance. You shall dwell in the land which I gave to your ancestors, and you shall be my people, and I will be your God (Ezek 36:26-28).

Until such time that God's ways are written in the center of our beings, we pray to be drawn into increasing congruity with God's Torah and the meaning of covenant. We struggle in prayer to understand what personal and communal responsibility entails. From the psalms, we learn that prayer is the intersecting of covenant partners—God and self and community—engaging in an ongoing process of finding a new song recognizably connected to and given life by the old.

Fourth, sometimes the "new song" sung by the psalmists is the old refashioned. A few of the psalms take up old patterns and fashion a new arrangement, a new prayer. Technically, this kind of prayer is called anthological. For instance, Psalm 33 reuses words or expressions from biblical wisdom (Prov 8:22-31; Sir 24). Psalm 6 borrows from Jeremiah. Psalm 79 is almost entirely anthological. Stuhlmueller shows that Psalm 79 shares in v. 1c a piece of Jer 26:18; in v. 4, Ps 44:13; in v. 5, Ps 89:46; in vv. 6-7, Jer 10:25; in v. 8d, Ps 142:6; in v. 9d, Pss 23:3, 25:11, 31:3; in v. 10a, Ps 115:2 and Joel 2:17; in v. 11, Ps 102:20; in v. 12, Ps 89:50-51; in v. 13a, Ps 100:3.[4] Psalm 86 draws even more heavily on other psalm texts. Stuhlmueller says of Psalm 86:

[4] Stuhlmueller, *Psalms 2,* 32.

This psalm manifests the power of memorized Bible texts for personal prayer. These passages, stored away in our subconscious, will spontaneously leap forward with God's direction and consolation for us, especially in times of distress. One text joined to another, especially in the context of daily life, will offer new insights, not anticipated ahead of time.[5]

Psalm 119, the longest psalm of the Psalter, also makes use of an anthological style, including among its many allusions citation of Deut 4:29 in v. 2; Isa 6:10 in v. 70; Isa 51:3 in v. 76; Jer 18:20 in v. 85; and Isa 40:8 in v. 89.[6] With the exception of v. 122, each of the 176 lines of Psalm 119 contains a synonym for the word "law." Stuhlmueller points out that the author "perhaps with wry humor" quotes from Deuteronomy, Proverbs, Job, Jeremiah, Ezekiel, and Isaiah 40–55, using "law" or its synonym in every line except one, but making "no allusions to the most important legal corpus in Israel, the Priestly Tradition or 'P' of the Pentateuch.'"[7]

Often anthological psalms do not allow us to conclude which text borrowed from which text or whether or not the authors were playfully repeating other texts. They do allow us to see at work in the practice of prayer the gathering up of the words of another and the transformation of these words in the arrangement of the borrowings. New prayers arise from the words of another. The repetitions in the anthological psalms suggest a practice we can incorporate in our own prayer by borrowing words from other prayers and arranging them in patterns of our own making that may alert us to new understandings of God, self, and community. Prayer need not be novel to be "new."

Stuhlmueller advocates memorized texts as a resource for prayer. This is surely a practice of the New Testament. Jesus quotes from Psalm 22 when on the cross he prays, "My God, my God, why have you forsaken me?" (Matt 27:46; Mark 15:34). For those whose biblical memory is not schooled or spontaneous, I would suggest a practice of prayer in which you copy those passages that express your sense of what it is you want to pray and arrange "your" verses in the way that seems suitable to your

---

[5] Ibid., 52. Stuhlmueller helpfully lists in tabular form the nineteen anthological repetitions in Psalm 86.

[6] For details, see Stuhlmueller, ibid., 152–155.

[7] Ibid., 152–153.

need. Reflect then on how your "new" prayer discloses your understanding of who God is for you and who you have sketched yourself or your community to be for God.

In some sense, this is a practice with which the Lectionary has already made us familiar. Rarely do we pray a psalm in its entire original arrangement in our liturgies. As a result often the church has written a new prayer by the deletion of verses and the arrangement of the psalm text. Corollary to this, we might develop the habit of noticing the deletion of verses from psalm texts in our liturgies and thus become aware of the altered meaning which can result from this practice.

Fifth, a "new song" will be increasingly possible for us as we grow in our familiarity with the psalm texts themselves. As a practice of prayer and study of the psalms, I suggest that you keep a journal in which you put into writing your reflections on the following:

1. *Imagined Author*—Before you read *about* a psalm, read the text itself with attentiveness to what it says. As an aid to this kind of close reading of the text, ask yourself who could have said words like these. From clues in the text itself, imagine an individual or a group who could have spoken the prayer you are reading. Record your insights.

2. *Imagined Life Situation*—Again from hints in the biblical text, ask yourself what kind of life experience could have occasioned the prayer you are considering. Use your imagination to picture a life setting for the psalmist. Imagine a particular experience occasioning the prayer. Do not be concerned about whether you are right or wrong about what you imagine. Simply test what you imagine from clues in the psalm itself. Does the text confirm what you are imagining?

3. *Psalm Type*—Note the type of psalm that you are considering. Is its content that of a hymn of praise, an enthronement psalm, a song of Zion, an individual or communal lament, a prayer of thanksgiving and trust, a royal psalm, a liturgical psalm, a wisdom psalm, or a mixed type prayer?[8]

4. *Literary/Theological Features*—Look closely for the poetic patterns which organize the psalm.[9] Note the expressions about God or the human family that catch your attention. What beliefs, atti-

---

[8] For particulars, review our discussion in CHAPTER 1.
[9] See our discussion in CHAPTER 2.

tudes, or practices in the psalm seem especially striking to you? Notice both positive and negative features that attract or repel you. Recognize that the psalms contain both comforting and disturbing theological features.

5. *Insights from Research*—Now look at a commentary and see what a scholar has found in the psalm you are considering. You might want to read what Carroll Stuhlmueller has said about your psalm in his two volume commentary in the Michael Glazier Old Testament Message series. In Stuhlmueller's *Psalms 1, 2*, the psalms are arranged in numerical order. Or you might want to consult Walter Brueggemann's *The Message of the Psalms*, which is arranged topically with a listing of the psalms treated at the end of the book. Additional commentaries and sources of study are listed and briefly described at the end of Stuhlmueller's *Psalms 2*. Some may find the brief commentary offered in *The New Jerome Biblical Commentary* especially useful.[10]

A benefit of keeping a journal on the psalms like the one described here is that in time as you repeat study of a psalm you will accumulate a body of information about the text. Insights from the scholars often shed new light on what you have already thought or suspected in your own analysis. Sometimes a scholar makes a comment that helps you understand what another scholar said. Close reading of the psalm texts themselves and reading of a number of scholars enlarges our appreciation and understanding of the psalm. From my own experience though, I urge you to study the psalm text *before* you turn to what the scholars have said about it so that the text itself has center place in the dialogue you have with the scholars.

6. *A Personal Statement*—Since this journal you are keeping can be an aid to prayer as well as to study, it is fitting to take time to write down your own prayer or feelings about the exercise of looking closely at a particular psalm. Record how your study of a psalm intersects with your understanding of God, self, and community. What prayer or conversation with God arises from your experience? What threads of connection do you see?

Sometimes the psalm takes us to a new threshold. We find our story in the prayer. We find that the words we need to speak

---

[10] *The New Jerome Biblical Commentary*, ed. Raymond E. Brown, S.S., Joseph A. Fitzmyer, S.J., Roland E. Murphy, O.Carm. (New Jersey: Englewood Cliffs, Prentice Hall, 1990). See especially John S. Kselman, S.S., and Michael L. Barre, S.S., "Psalms," 523–552.

spring to our heart. Do not shy away from identifying where you are on your own journey. Speak boldly! Prayer is a process of maintaining tradition. Dialogue with God is one way to attend to the work of choosing a direction and of committing to move purposefully on a path that leads to our hearts' desire. Prayer helps us name our reality. Prayer, as the psalms teach, can change things.

A CLOSING WORD

Our study began with "A Prayer for Proceeding" in the spirit of Psalm 8. We shall end with a prayer in the spirit of Psalm 144, an anthological psalm that incorporates lines and phrases from Ps 18:2, 4, 9, 14, 16, with an allusion to the dignity of humanity reminiscent of Psalm 8. With Psalm 144:9, we join in "singing a new song" to God. With words as our sacrifice (Ps 141:2), let us continue to study and to pray.

A PRAYER FOR GOING ON

Accept, O God, our prayer as incense before you, and the lifting up of our hands as the evening sacrifice. Broken hearted and joyful, let us come before you, Holy Source of life. Cause us to see your living presence that we might know you better and so learn to know ourselves more fully with no shame.

Cultivate in us sensitivity to your time and your space. Be with us as we choose directions and take steps to find our way. Alert us to your stirring in our hearts.

> Blessed be you, O YHWH, our rock,
>   for freeing us to voice the matters of our hearts.
> You are a Holy God, our fortress,
>   our courage and our deliverer,
>   our shield in whom we take shelter.

O YHWH, who are we that you have regard for us,
   mere human beings that you do care for us?
We are like a breath,
   our days are like a passing shadow.

O YHWH, bend your sky and come down;
   touch the mountains and they will smoke.
Reach your hand down from on high;
   rescue us and deliver us from the mighty waters,
   from the hands of those whose mouths speak lies
   and whose oaths are false.

O YHWH, we will sing a new song to you,
   play for you upon a ten-stringed harp,
   pray to you with breath within your breath.
Allow our hearts to believe, hope, and trust.
Be with us, deliver us, hold out to us a good future.
Cast fear, chaos, and indecision far from us.

Happy the people to whom such blessings fall!
Happy the people who trust in YHWH!

Appendix A
LORD

YHWH (or some form of this name) and Adon (or some form of
this name, a title of courtesy often substituted for the divine name)
appear 803 times in the Book of Psalms with 798 references to
the God of Israel and 5 references to other(s) as god(s) or human
lord(s) or master(s). For discussion, see 91–95.

English Word/ Hebrew Word	Transliteration	BHS Frequency
LORD		
יהוה	YHWH (pr.n.)	689 occurrences
יָהּ	YaH (pr.n.)	43 occurrences
GOD	YHWH with vowels	6 occurrences
יְהוִה	of Elohim	
		738 occurrences
Lord/lord(s)		
אָרוֹן	Adon (n.m.s.)	4 occurrences
אֲדֹנָי	Adonay (n.m.p.-1 c.s. sf.)	54 occurrences
אֲדֹנַיִךְ	Adonayik (n.m.p.-2 f.s. sf.)	1 occurrence
אֲדֹנֵי	Adone (n.m.p. cstr.)	1 occurrence
אֲדֹנֵינוּ	Adonenu (n.m.p.-1 c.p. sf.)	3 occurrences
אֲדֹנִי	Adoni (n.m.s.-1 c.s. sf.)	1 occurrence
אֲדֹנִים	Adonim (n.m.p.)	1 occurrence
		65 occurrences
		TOTAL 803 occurrences

Five References to other god(s) or human master(s):
Pss 12:4; 45:11; 105:21; 110:1; 136:3

Abbreviations:

c.	common	m.	masculine	paus.	pausal
cstr.	construct	n.	noun	s.	singular
f.	feminine	p.	plural	sf.	suffix

692 Occurrences of LORD in Revised Standard Version
689 Occurrences of YHWH in Biblia Hebraica Stuttgartensia
(the standard Hebrew Bible text)
—Signals same verse listing in RSV and BHS

RSV	BHS	RSV	BHS	RSV	BHS
1. 1.2	—	31. 7.0	7.1	61. 12.3	12.4
2. 1.6	—	32. 7.1	7.2	62. 12.5	12.6
3. 2.2	—	33. 7.3	7.4	63. 12.6	12.7
4. 2.4	Not in BHS	34. 7.6	7.7	64. 12.7	12.8
5. 2.7	—	35. 7.8	7.9	65. 13.1	13.2
6. 2.11	—	36. 7.8	7.9	66. 13.3	13.4
7. 3.1	3.2	37. 7.17	7.18	67. 13.6	—
8. 3.3	3.4	38. 7.17	7.18	68. 14.2	—
9. 3.4	3.5	39. 8.1	8.2	69. 14.4	—
10. 3.5	3.6	40. 8.9	8.10	70. 14.6	—
11. 3.7	3.8	41. 9.1	9.2	71. 14.7	—
12. 3.8	3.9	42. 9.7	9.8	72. 15.1	—
13. 4.3	4.4	43. 9.9	9.10	73. 15.4	—
14. 4.3	4.4	44. 9.10	9.11	74. 16.2	—
15. 4.5	4.6	45. 9.11	9.12	75. 16.5	—
16. 4.6	4.7	46. 9.13	9.14	76. 16.7	—
17. 4.8	4.9	47. 9.16	9.17	77. 16.8	—
18. 5.1	5.2	48. 9.19	9.20	78. 17.1	—
19. 5.3	5.4	49. 9.20	9.21	79. 17.13	—
20. 5.6	5.7	50. 10.1	—	80. 17.14	—
21. 5.8	5.9	51. 10.3	—	81. 18.0	18.1
22. 5.12	5.13	52. 10.12	—	82. 18.0	18.1
23. 6.1	6.2	53. 10.16	—	83. 18.0	18.1
24. 6.2	6.3	54. 10.17	—	84. 18.1	18.2
25. 6.2	6.3	55. 11.1	—	85. 18.2	18.3
26. 6.3	6.4	56. 11.4	—	86. 18.3	18.4
27. 6.4	6.5	57. 11.4	—	87. 18.6	18.7
28. 6.8	6.9	58. 11.5	—	88. 18.13	18.14
29. 6.9	6.10	59. 11.7	—	89. 18.15	18.16
30. 6.9	6.10	60. 12.1	—	90. 18.18	18.19

	RSV	BHS		RSV	BHS		RSV	BHS
91.	18.20	18.21	126.	24.5	—	161.	28.6	—
92.	18.21	18.22	127.	24.8	—	162.	28.7	—
93.	18.24	18.25	128.	24.8	—	163.	28.8	—
94.	18.28	18.29	129.	24.10	—	164.	29.1	—
95.	18.30	18.31	130.	25.1	—	165.	29.1	—
96.	18.31	18.32	131.	25.4	—	166.	29.2	—
97.	18.41	18.42	132.	24.6	—	167.	29.2	—
98.	18.46	18.47	133.	25.7	—	168.	29.3	—
99.	18.49	18.50	134.	25.8	—	169.	29.3	—
100.	19.7	19.8	135.	25.10	—	170.	29.4	—
101.	19.7	19.8	136.	25.11	—	171.	29.4	—
102.	19.8	19.9	137.	25.12	—	172.	29.5	—
103.	19.8	19.9	138.	25.14	—	173.	29.5	—
104.	19.9	19.10	139.	25.15	—	174.	29.7	—
105.	19.9	19.10	140.	26.1	—	175.	29.8	—
106.	19.14	19.15	141.	26.1	—	176.	29.8	—
107.	20.1	20.2	142.	26.2	—	177.	29.9	—
108.	20.5	20.6	143.	26.6	—	178.	29.10	—
109.	20.6	20.7	144.	26.8	—	179.	29.10	—
110.	20.7	20.8	145.	26.12	—	180.	29.11	—
111.	20.9	20.10	146.	27.1	—	181.	29.11	—
112.	21.1	21.2	147.	27.1	—	182.	30.1	30.2
113.	21.7	21.8	148.	27.4	—	183.	30.2	30.3
114.	21.9	21.10	149.	27.4	—	184.	30.3	30.4
115.	21.13	21.14	150.	27.4	—	185.	30.7	30.8
116.	22.8	22.9	151.	27.6	—	186.	30.8	30.9
117.	22.19	22.20	152.	27.7	—	187.	30.8	Not in BHS
118.	22.23	22.24	153.	27.8	—	188.	30.10	30.11
119.	22.26	22.27	154.	27.10	—	189.	30.10	30.11
120.	22.27	22.28	155.	27.11	—	190.	30.12	30.13
121.	22.28	22.29	156.	27.13	—	191.	31.1	31.2
122.	23.1	—	157.	27.14	—	192.	31.5	31.6
123.	23.6	—	158.	27.14	—	193.	31.6	31.7
124.	24.1	—	159.	28.1	—	194.	31.9	31.10
125.	24.3	—	160.	28.5	—	195.	31.14	31.15

RSV	BHS	RSV	BHS	RSV	BHS
196. 31.17	31.18	231. 34.18	34.19	266. 39.4	39.5
197. 31.21	31.22	232. 34.19	34.20	267. 39.12	39.13
198. 31.23	31.24	233. 34.22	34.23	268. 40.1	40.2
199. 31.23	31.24	234. 35.1	—	269. 40.3	40.4
200. 31.24	31.25	235. 35.5	—	270. 40.4	40.5
201. 32.2	—	236. 35.6	—	271. 40.5	40.6
202. 32.5	—	237. 35.9	—	272. 40.9	40.10
203. 32.10	—	238. 35.10	—	273. 40.11	40.12
204. 32.11	—	239. 35.17	Not in BHS	274. 40.13	40.14
205. 33.1	—	240. 35.22	—	275. 40.13	40.14
206. 33.2	—	241. 35.24	—	276. 40.16	40.17
207. 33.4	—	242. 35.27	—	277. 41.1	41.2
208. 33.5	—	243. 36.0	36.1	278. 41.2	41.3
209. 33.6	—	244. 36.5	36.6	279. 41.3	41.4
210. 33.8	—	245. 36.6	36.7	280. 41.4	41.5
211. 33.10	—	246. 37.3	—	281. 41.10	41.11
212. 33.11	—	247. 37.4	—	282. 41.13	41.14
213. 33.12	—	248. 37.5	—	283. 42.8	42.9
214. 33.13	—	249. 37.7	—	284. 46.7	46.8
215. 33.18	—	250. 37.9	—	285. 46.8	46.9
216. 33.20	—	251. 37.13	Not in BHS	286. 46.11	46.12
217. 33.22	—	252. 37.17	—	287. 47.2	47.3
218. 34.1	34.2	253. 37.18	—	288. 47.5	47.6
219. 34.2	34.3	254. 37.20	—	289. 48.1	48.2
220. 34.3	34.4	255. 37.23	—	290. 48.8	48.9
221. 34.4	34.5	256. 37.24	—	291. 50.1	—
222. 34.6	34.7	257. 37.28	—	292. 54.6	54.8
223. 34.7	34.8	258. 37.33	—	293. 55.16	55.17
224. 34.8	34.9	259. 37.34	—	294. 55.22	55.23
225. 34.9	34.10	260. 37.39	—	295. 56.10	56.11
226. 34.10	34.11	261. 37.40	—	296. 58.6	58.7
227. 34.11	34.12	262. 38.1	38.2	297. 59.3	59.4
228. 34.15	34.16	263. 38.15	38.16	298. 59.5	59.6
229. 34.16	34.17	264. 38.15	Not in BHS	299. 59.8	59.9
230. 34.17	34.18	265. 38.21	38.22	300. 64.10	64.11

RSV	BHS	RSV	BHS	RSV	BHS
301. 68.16	68.17	336. 86.6	—	371. 94.3	—
302. 68.26	68.27	337. 86.11	—	372. 94.5	—
303. 69.13	69.14	338. 86.17	—	373. 94.11	—
304. 69.16	69.17	339. 87.2	—	374. 94.14	—
305. 69.31	69.32	340. 87.6	—	375. 94.17	—
306. 69.33	69.34	341. 88.1	88.2	376. 94.18	—
307. 70.1	70.2	342. 88.9	88.10	377. 94.22	—
308. 70.5	70.6	343. 88.13	88.14	378. 94.23	—
309. 71.1	—	344. 88.14	88.15	379. 95.1	—
310. 71.5	—	345. 89.1	89.2	380. 95.3	—
311. 72.18	—	346. 89.5	89.6	381. 95.6	—
312. 74.18	—	347. 89.6	89.7	382. 96.1	—
313. 75.8	75.9	348. 89.6	89.7	383. 96.2	—
314. 76.11	76.12	349. 89.9	—	384. 96.4	—
315. 78.4	—	350. 89.15	89.16	385. 96.5	—
316. 78.21	—	351. 89.18	89.19	386. 96.7	—
317. 79.5	—	352. 89.46	89.47	387. 96.7	—
318. 80.4	80.5	353. 89.51	89.52	388. 96.8	—
319. 80.19	80.20	354. 89.52	89.53	389. 96.9	—
320. 81.10	81.11	355. 90.13	—	390. 96.10	—
321. 81.15	81.16	356. 91.2	—	391. 96.13	—
322. 83.16	83.17	357. 91.9	—	392. 97.1	—
323. 83.18	83.19	358. 92.1	92.2	393. 97.5	—
324. 84.1	84.2	359. 92.4	92.5	394. Not in RSV	97.8
325. 84.2	84.3	360. 92.5	92.6	395. 97.9	—
326. 84.3	84.4	361. 92.8	92.9	396. 97.10	—
327. 84.8	84.9	362. 92.9	92.10	397. 97.12	—
328. 84.11	84.12	363. 92.13	92.14	398. 98.1	—
329. 84.11	84.12	364. 92.15	92.16	399. 98.2	—
330. 84.12	84.13	365. 93.1	—	400. 98.4	—
331. 85.1	85.2	366. 93.1	—	401. 98.5	—
332. 85.7	85.8	367. 93.3	—	402. 98.6	—
333. 85.8	85.9	368. 93.4	—	403. 98.9	—
334. 85.12	85.13	369. 93.5	—	404. 99.1	—
335. 86.1	—	370. 94.1	—	405. 99.2	—

RSV	BHS	RSV	BHS	RSV	BHS
406. 99.5	—	441. 104.31	—	476. 109.27	—
407. 99.6	—	442. 104.33	—	477. 109.30	—
408. 99.8	—	443. 104.34	—	478. 110.1	—
409. 99.9	—	444. 104.35	—	479. 110.2	—
410. 99.9	—	445. 105.1	—	480. 110.4	—
411. 100.1	—	446. 105.3	—	481. 111.1	—
412. 100.2	—	447. 105.4	—	482. 111.2	—
413. 100.3	—	448. 105.7	—	483. 111.4	—
414. 100.5	—	449. 105.19	—	484. 111.10	111.11
415. 101.1	—	450. 106.1	—	485. 112.1	—
416. 101.8	—	451. 106.2	—	486. 112.7	—
417. 102.0	102.1	452. 106.4	—	487. 113.1	—
418. 102.1	102.2	453. 106.16	—	488. 113.1	—
419. 102.12	102.13	454. 106.25	—	489. 113.2	—
420. 102.15	102.16	455. 106.34	—	490. 113.3	—
421. 102.16	102.17	456. 106.40	—	491. 113.4	—
422. 102.19	102.20	457. 106.47	—	492. 113.5	—
423. 102.21	102.22	458. 106.48	—	493. 115.1	—
424. 102.22	102.23	459. 107.1	—	494. 115.9	—
425. 103.1	—	460. 107.2	—	495. 115.10	—
426. 103.2	—	461. 107.6	—	496. 115.11	—
427. 103.6	—	462. 107.8	—	497. 115.11	—
428. 103.8	—	463. 107.13	—	498. 115.12	—
429. 103.13	—	464. 107.15	—	499. 115.13	—
430. 103.17	—	465. 107.19	—	500. 115.14	—
431. 103.19	—	466. 107.21	—	501. 115.15	—
432. 103.20	—	467. 107.24	—	502. 115.16	—
433. 103.21	—	468. 107.28	—	503. 116.1	—
434. 103.22	—	469. 107.31	—	504. 116.4	—
435. 103.22	—	470. 107.43	—	505. 116.4	—
436. 104.1	—	471. 108.3	108.4	506. 116.5	—
437. 104.1	—	472. 109.14	—	507. 116.6	—
438. 104.16	—	473. 109.15	—	508. 116.7	—
439. 104.24	—	474. 109.20	—	509. 116.9	—
440. 104.31	—	475. 109.26	—	510. 116.12	—

RSV	BHS	RSV	BHS	RSV	BHS
511. 116.13	—	546. 119.31	—	581. 124.2	—
512. 116.14	—	547. 119.33	—	582. 124.6	—
513. 116.15	—	548. 119.41	—	583. 124.8	—
514. 116.16	—	549. 119.52	—	584. 125.1	—
515. 116.17	—	550. 119.55	—	585. 125.2	—
516. 116.18	—	551. 119.57	—	586. 125.4	—
517. 116.19	—	552. 119.64	—	587. 125.5	—
518. 117.1	—	553. 119.65	—	588. 126.1	—
519. 117.2	—	554. 119.75	—	589. 126.2	—
520. 118.1	—	555. 119.89	—	590. 126.3	—
521. 118.4	—	556. 119.107	—	591. 126.4	—
522. 118.5	—	557. 119.108	—	592. 127.1	—
523. 118.5	—	558. 119.126	—	593. 127.1	—
524. 118.6	—	559. 119.137	—	594. 127.3	—
525. 118.7	—	560. 119.145	—	595. 128.1	—
526. 118.8	—	561. 119.149	—	596. 128.4	—
527. 118.9	—	562. 119.151	—	597. 128.5	—
528. 118.10	—	563. 119.156	—	598. 129.4	—
529. 118.11	—	564. Not in RSV	119.159	599. 129.8	—
530. 118.12	—	565. 119.166	—	600. 129.8	—
531. 118.13	—	566. 119.169	—	601. 130.1	—
532. 118.15	—	567. 119.174	—	602. 130.5	—
533. 118.16	—	568. 120.1	—	603. 130.7	—
534. 118.16	—	569. 120.2	—	604. 130.7	—
535. 118.20	—	570. 121.2	—	605. 131.1	—
536. 118.23	—	571. 121.5	—	606. 131.3	—
537. 118.24	—	572. 121.5	—	607. 132.1	—
538. 118.25	—	573. 121.7	—	608. 132.2	—
539. 118.25	—	574. 121.8	—	609. 132.5	—
540. 118.26	—	575. 122.1	—	610. 132.8	—
541. 118.26	—	576. 122.4	—	611. 132.11	—
542. 118.27	—	577. 122.9	—	612. 132.13	—
543. 118.29	—	578. 123.2	—	613. 133.3	—
544. 119.1	—	579. 123.3	—	614. 134.1	—
545. 119.12	—	580. 124.1	—	615. 134.1	—

	RSV	BHS		RSV	BHS		RSV	BHS
616.	134.1	—	651.	140.8	140.9	686.	147.7	—
617.	134.2	—	652.	140.12	140.13	687.	147.11	—
618.	134.3	—	653.	141.1	—	688.	147.12	—
619.	135.1	—	654.	141.3	—	689.	148.1	—
620.	135.1	—	655.	142.1	142.2	690.	148.5	—
621.	135.2	—	656.	142.1	142.2	691.	148.7	—
622.	135.3	—	657.	142.5	142.6	692.	148.13	—
623.	135.5	—	658.	143.1	—	693.	149.1	—
624.	135.6	—	659.	143.7	—	694.	149.4	—
625.	135.13	—	660.	143.9	—			
626.	135.13	—	661.	143.11	—			
627.	135.14	—	662.	144.1	—			
628.	135.19	—	663.	144.3	—			
629.	135.19	—	664.	144.5	—			
630.	135.20	—	665.	144.15	—			
631.	135.20	—	666.	145.3	—			
632.	135.20	—	667.	145.8	—			
633.	135.21	—	668.	145.9	—			
634.	136.1	—	669.	145.10	—			
635.	137.4	—	670.	145.14	—			
636.	137.7	—	671.	145.17	—			
637.	138.4	—	672.	145.18	—			
638.	138.5	—	673.	145.20	—			
639.	138.5	—	674.	145.21	—			
640.	138.6	—	675.	146.1	—			
641.	138.8	—	676.	146.2	—			
642.	138.8	—	677.	146.5	—			
643.	139.1	—	678.	146.7	—			
644.	139.4	—	679.	146.8	—			
645.	139.21	—	680.	146.8	—			
646.	140.1	140.2	681.	146.8	—			
647.	140.4	140.5	682.	146.9	—			
648.	140.6	140.7	683.	146.10	—			
649.	140.6	140.7	684.	147.2	—			
650.	140.7	140.8	685.	147.6	—			

43 Occurrences of LORD in Revised Standard Version as YaH in Biblia Hebraica Stuttgartensia

RSV	BHS		RSV	BHS		RSV	BHS
1. 68.4	68.5	15.	113.9	—	29.	135.1	—
2. 68.18	68.19	16.	115.17	—	30.	135.3	—
3. 77.11	77.12	17.	115.18	—	31.	135.4	—
4. 89.8	89.9	18.	115.18	—	32.	135.21	—
5. 94.7	—	19.	116.19	—	33.	146.1	—
6. 94.12	—	20.	117.2	—	34.	146.10	—
7. 102.18	102.19	21.	118.5	—	35.	147.1	—
8. 104.35	—	22.	118.5	—	36.	147.20	—
9. 105.45	—	23.	118.14	—	37.	148.1	—
10. 106.1	—	24.	118.17	—	38.	148.14	—
11. 106.48	—	25.	118.18	—	39.	149.1	—
12. 111.1	—	26.	118.19	—	40.	149.9	—
13. 112.1	—	27.	122.4	—	41.	150.1	—
14. 113.1	—	28.	130.3	—	42.	150.6	—
					43.	150.6	—

6 Occurrences of GOD in Revised Standard Version as YHWH with vowels of Elohim in Biblia Hebraica Stuttgartensia

	RSV	BHS
1.	68.20	68.21
2.	69.6	69.7
3.	71.16	—
4.	73.28	—
5.	109.21	—
6.	141.8	—

Occurrences of Forms of Lord in
Revised Standard Version and Biblia Hebraica Stuttgartensia.
Notation [human] or [other gods] added to the five verses that
do not refer to the God of Israel.

Adon (Lord or lord)

	RSV	BHS		RSV	BHS		RSV	BHS
			21.	66.18	—	53.	140.7	140.8
1.	12.4 [human]	12.5	22.	68.11	68.12	54.	141.8	—
			23.	68.17	68.18			
2.	97.5	—	24.	68.19	68.20			
3.	105.21 [human]	—	25.	68.20	68.21			
			26.	68.22	68.23			
4.	114.7	—	27.	68.32	68.33			
			28.	69.6	69.7			

Adonayik (your lord)

	RSV	BHS
1.	45.11 [human]	45.12

Adonay (Lord or my Lord)

	RSV	BHS		RSV	BHS
			29.	71.5	—
1.	Not in RSV	2.4	30.	71.16	—
2.	16.2		31.	Not in RSV	73.20
3.	22.30	22.31	32.	73.28	—
4.	Not in RSV	30.9	33.	77.2	77.3
5.	Not in RSV	35.17	34.	77.7	77.8
6.	35.22	—	35.	78.65	—
7.	35.23	—	36.	79.12	—
8.	Not in RSV	37.13	37.	86.3	—
9.	38.9	38.10	38.	86.4	—
10.	Not in RSV	38.16	39.	86.5	—
11.	38.22	38.23	40.	86.8	—
12.	39.7	39.8	41.	86.9	—
13.	40.17	40.18	42.	86.12	—
14.	44.23	44.24	43.	86.15	—
15.	51.15	51.17	44.	89.49	89.50
16.	54.4	54.6	45.	89.50	89.51
17.	55.9	55.10	46.	90.1	—
18.	57.9	57.10	47.	90.17	
19.	59.11	59.12	48.	109.21	—
20.	62.12	62.13	49.	110.5	—
			50.	130.2	—
			51.	130.3	—
			52.	130.6	—

Adone (Lord of)

	RSV	BHS
1.	136.3	—

Adonenu (our Lord)

	RSV	BHS
1.	8.2	—
2.	8.9	8.10
3.	135.5	—

Adoni (my lord)

	RSV	BHS
1.	110.1 [human]	—

Adonim (lords)

	RSV	BHS
1.	136.3 [other gods]	—

Appendix B
God

Elohim and El (or some form of these names) appear 440 times in the Book of Psalms with 428 references to the God of Israel and 12 references to other gods. For discussion, see pp. 95–98.

Hebrew Word	Transliteration	BHS Frequency
אֱלֹהִים	Elohim (n.m.p.)	240 occurrences
אֵל	El (n.m.s.)	61 occurrences
אֵלַי	Elay (n.m.s.-1 c.s. sf.)	1 occurrence
אֵלִי	Eli (n.m.s.-1 c.s. sf.)	10 occurrences
אֱלֹהַּ	Eloha (n.m.s.-1 c.s. sf. paus.)	16 occurrences
אֱלֹהַי	Elohay (n.m.p.-1 c.s. sf.)	30 occurrences
אֱלֹהֵי	Elohe (n.m.p. cstr.)	33 occurrences
אֱלֹהֵיהֶם	Elohehem (n.m.p.-3.m.p. sf.)	2 occurrences
אֱלֹהָיו	Elohaw (n.m.p.-3.m.s. sf.)	4 occurrences
אֱלֹהַיִךְ	Elohayik (n.m.p.-2 f.s. sf.)	2 occurrences
אֱלֹהֶיךָ	Eloheka (n.m.p.-2 m.s. sf.)	6 occurrences
אֱלֹהֵיכֶם	Elohekem (n.m.p.-2 m.p. sf.)	1 occurrence
אֱלֹהֵינוּ	Elohenu (n.m.p.-1 c.p. sf.)	30 occurrences
אֱלוֹהַּ	Eloah (n.m.s.)	4 occurrences

TOTAL 440 occurrences

Twelve References to other gods:
Elohim—Pss 82:1, 6; 84:7; 86:8; 95:3; 96:4;
          97:7, 9; 135:5; 136:2; 138:1
Elohe—Ps 96:5

239 Occurrences of God in Revised Standard Version
240 Occurrences of Elohim in Biblia Hebraica Stuttgartensia

RSV	BHS		RSV	BHS		RSV	BHS
1. 3.2	3.3	32.	45.7	45.8	63.	51.17	51.19
2. 5.10	5.11	33.	46.1	46.2	64.	52.7	52.9
3. 7.9	7.10	34.	46.4	46.5	65.	52.8	52.9
4. 7.10	7.11	35.	46.5	46.6	66.	52.8	52.10
5. 7.11	7.12	36.	46.5	46.6	67.	53.1	53.2
6. 8.5	8.6	37.	46.10	46.11	68.	53.2	53.3
7. 9.17	9.18	38.	47.1	47.2	69.	53.2	53.3
8. 10.4	—	39.	47.5	47.6	70.	53.4	53.5
9. 10.13	—	40.	47.6	47.7	71.	53.5	53.6
10. 14.1	—	41.	47.7	47.8	72.	53.5	53.6
11. 14.2	—	42.	47.8	47.9	73.	53.6	53.7
12. 14.5	—	43.	47.8	47.9	74.	54.1	54.3
13. 25.22	—	44.	47.9	47.10	75.	54.2	54.4
14. 36.1	36.2	45.	48.3	48.4	76.	54.3	54.5
15. 36.7	36.8	46.	48.8	48.9	77.	54.4	54.6
16. 42.1	42.2	47.	48.9	48.10	78.	55.1	55.2
17. 42.2	42.3	48.	48.10	48.11	79.	55.14	55.15
18. 42.2	42.3	49.	48.14	48.15	80.	55.19	55.20
19. 42.4	42.5	50.	49.7	49.8	81.	55.23	55.24
20. 42.5	42.6	51.	49.15	49.16	82.	56.1	56.2
21. 42.11	42.12	52.	50.1	—	83.	56.4	56.5
22. 43.1	—	53.	50.2	—	84.	56.4	56.5
23. 43.4	—	54.	50.6	—	85.	56.7	56.8
24. 43.4	—	55.	50.7	—	86.	56.9	56.10
25. 43.5	—	56.	50.14	—	87.	56.10	56.11
26. 44.1	44.2	57.	50.16	—	88.	56.11	56.12
27. 44.4	44.5	58.	50.23	—	89.	56.12	56.13
28. 44.8	44.9	59.	51.1	51.3	90.	56.13	56.14
29. 44.21	44.22	60.	51.10	51.12	91.	57.1	57.2
30. 45.2	45.3	61.	51.14	51.16	92.	57.2	57.3
31. 45.6	45.7	62.	51.17	51.19	93.	57.3	57.4

RSV	BHS	RSV	BHS	RSV	BHS
94. 57.5	57.6	129. 66.10	—	164. 69.13	69.14
95. 57.7	57.8	130. 66.16	—	165. 69.29	69.30
96. 57.11	57.12	131. 66.19	—	166 69.30	69.31
97. 58.6	58.7	132. 66.20	—	167. 69.32	69.33
98. 58.11	58.12	133. 67.1	67.2	168. 69.35	69.36
99. 59.5	59.6	134. 67.3	67.4	169. 70.1	70.2
100. 59.9	59.10	135. 67.5	67.6	170. 70.4	70.5
101. 59.10	59.11	136. 67.6	67.7	171 70.5	70.6
102. 59.13	59.14	137. 67.7	67.8	172. 71.11	—
103. 59.17	59.18	138. 68.1	68.2	173. 71.12	—
104. 60.1	60.3	139. 68.2	68.3	174. 71.17	—
105. 60.6	60.8	140. 68.3	68.4	175. 71.18	—
106. 60.10	60.12	141. 68.4	68.5	176. 71.19	—
107. 60.10	60.12	142. 68.5	68.6	177. 71.19	—
108. 60.12	60.14	143. 68.6	68.7	178. 72.1	—
109. 61.1	61.2	144. 68.7	68.8	179. 72.18	—
110. 61.5	61.6	145. 68.8	68.9	180. 73.1	—
111. 61.7	61.8	146. 68.8	68.9	181. 73.26	—
112. 62.1	62.2	147. 68.9	68.10	182. 73.28	—
113. 62.5	62.6	148. 68.10	68.11	183. 74.1	—
114. 62.7	62.8	149. Not in RSV	68.16	184. 74.10	—
115. 62.7	62.8	150. 68.16	68.17	185. 74.12	—
116. 62.8	62.9	151. Not in RSV	68.18	186. 74.22	—
117. 62.11	62.12	152. 68.18	68.19	187. 75.1	75.2
118. 62.11	62.12	153. 68.21	68.22	188. 75.7	75.8
119. 63.1	63.2	154. 68.24	68.25	189. 76.1	76.2
120. 63.11	63.12	155. 68.26	68.27	190. 76.9	76.10
121. 64.1	64.2	156. 68.28	68.29	191. 77.1	77.2
122. 64.7	64.8	157. 68.31	68.32	192. 77.3	77.4
123. 64.9	64.10	158. 68.32	68.33	193. 77.13	77.14
124. 65.1	65.2	159. 68.34	68.35	194. 77.13	77.14
125. 65.9	65.10	160. 68.35	68.36	195. 77.16	77.17
126. 66.1	—	161 68.35	68.36	196. 78.7	—
127. 66.3	—	162. 69.1	69.2	197. 78.10	—
128. 66.5	—	163. 69.5	69.6	198. 78.19	—

RSV	BHS	RSV	BHS	RSV	BHS
199. 78.22	—	234. 108.7	108.8	24. 68.20	68.21
200. 78.31	—	235. 108.11	108.12	25. 68.35	68.36
201. 78.35	—	236. 108.11	108.12	26. 73.11	—
202. 78.56	—	237. 108.13	108.14	27. 73.17	—
203. 78.59	—	238. 135.5	—	28. 74.8	—
204. 79.1	—	239. 136.2	—	29. 77.9	77.10
205. 80.3	80.4	240. 138.1	—	30. 77.13	77.14
206. 80.4	80.5	241. 144.9	—	31. 77.14	77.15
207. 80.7	80.8			32. 78.7	—
208. 80.14	80.15			33. 78.8	—
209. 80.19	80.20	**El**		34. 78.18	—
210. 81.1	81.2	**RSV**	**BHS**	35. 78.19	—
211. 82.1	—	1. 5.4	5.5	36. 78.34	—
212. 82.1	—	2. 7.11	7.12	37. 78.35	—
213. 82.6	—	3. 10.11	—	38. 81.9	81.10
214. 82.8	—	4. 10.12	—	39. 81.9	81.10
215. 83.1	83.2	5. 16.1	—	40. 83.1	83.2
216. 83.12	83.13	6. 17.6	—	41. 84.2	84.3
217. 84.7	84.8	7. 18.30	18.31	42. 84.7	84.8
218. 84.8	84.9	8. 18.32	18.33	43. 85.8	85.9
219. 84.9	84.10	9. 18.47	18.48	44. 86.15	—
220. 84.11	84.12	10. 19.1	19.2	45. 89.7	89.8
221. 86.8	—	11. 29.3	—	46. 90.2	—
222. 86.10	—	12. 31.5	31.6	47. 94.1	—
223. 86.14	—	13. 36.6	36.7	48. 94.1	—
224. 87.3	—	14. 44.20	44.21	49. 95.3	—
225. 90.0	90.1	15. 42.2	42.3	50. 99.8	—
226. 95.3	—	16. 42.8	42.9	51. 104.21	—
227. 96.4	—	17. 42.9	42.10	52. 106.14	—
228. 97.7	—	18. 43.4	—	53. 106.21	—
229. 97.8	Not in BHS	19. 52.5	52.7	54. 107.11	—
230. 97.9	—	20. 55.19	55.20	55. 118.27	—
231. 100.3	—	21. 57.2	57.3	56. 136.26	—
232. 108.1	108.2	22. 68.19	68.20	57. 139.17	—
233. 108.5	108.6	23. 68.20	68.21	58. 139.23	—

	RSV	BHS		RSV	BHS		RSV	BHS
59.	146.5	—	13.	84.3	84.4	29.	145.1	—
60.	149.6	—	14.	109.26	—	30.	146.2	—
61.	150.1	—	15.	119.115	—			
			16.	143.10	—			

Elay (my God or for me)

Elohe (God/gods of)

	RSV	BHS					RSV	BHS
1.	7.6	7.7				1.	4.1	4.2
						2.	18.46	18.47

Eli (my God)

Elohay (my God)

	RSV	BHS		RSV	BHS		RSV	BHS
			1.	3.7	3.8	3.	20.1	20.2
1.	18.2	18.3	2.	7.1	7.2	4.	24.5	—
2.	22.1	22.2	3.	7.3	7.4	5.	25.5	—
3.	22.1	22.2	4.	18.6	18.7	6.	27.9	—
4.	22.10	22.11	5.	18.28	18.29	7.	41.13	41.14
5.	63.1	63.2	6.	18.29	18.30	8.	43.2	—
6.	68.24	68.25	7.	22.2	22.3	9.	46.7	46.8
7.	89.26	89.27	8.	25.2	—	10.	46.11	46.12
8.	102.24	102.25	9.	30.12	30.13	11.	47.9	47.10
9.	118.28	—	10.	31.14	31.15	12.	51.14	51.16
10.	140.6	140.7	11.	35.23	—	13.	59.5	59.6
			12.	38.21	38.22	14.	59.10	59.11
			13.	40.5	40.6	15.	59.17	59.18
			14.	40.8	40.9	16.	65.5	65.6

Eloha (my God)

	RSV	BHS		RSV	BHS		RSV	BHS
			15.	40.17	40.18	17.	68.8	68.9
1.	5.2	5.3	16.	42.6	42.7	18.	69.6	69.7
2.	13.3	13.4	17.	59.10	59.11	19.	72.18	—
3.	18.21	18.22	18.	71.4	—	20.	75.9	75.10
4.	30.2	30.3	19.	71.12	—	21.	76.6	76.7
5.	35.24	—	20.	83.13	83.14	22.	79.9	—
6.	38.15	38.16	21.	84.10	84.11	23.	81.1	81.2
7.	42.11	42.12	22.	86.2	—	24.	81.4	—
8.	43.4	—	23.	86.12	—	25.	84.8	84.9
9.	43.5	—	24.	91.2	—	26.	85.4	85.5
10.	59.1	59.2	25.	94.22	—	27.	88.1	88.2
11.	69.3	69.4	26.	104.1	—	28.	89.8	89.9
12.	71.22	—	27.	104.33	—	29.	94.7	—
			28.	118.28	—	30.	96.5	—

RSV	BHS		RSV	BHS
31. 106.48	—	3. 20.07	20.08
32. 109.1	—	4. 40.03	40.04
33. 136.2	—	5. 44.20	44.21
		6. 48.1	48.2

Elohehem (their God)

		7. 48.8	48.9

RSV	BHS		8. 48.14	48.15
1. 79.10	—	9. 50.3	—
2. 115.2	—	10. 66.8	—
		11. 67.6	67.7

Elohaw (his God)

		12. 90.17	—
1. 33.12	—	13. 92.13	92.14
2. 37.31	—	14. 94.23	—
3. 144.15	—	15. 95.7	—
4. 146.5	—	16. 98.3	—
		17. 99.5	—

Elohayik (your God)

		18. 99.8	—
1. 146.10	—	19. 99.9	—
2. 147.12	—	20. 99.9	—
		21. 105.7	—

Eloheka (your God)

		22. 106.47	—
1. 42.3	42.4	23. 113.5	—
2. 42.10	42.11	24. 115.3	—
3. 45.7	45.8	25. 116.5	—
4. 50.7	—	26. 122.9	—
5. 68.28	68.29	27. 123.2	—
6. 81.10	81.11	28. 135.2	—
		29. 147.1	—

Elohekem (your God) 30. 147.1 —

RSV	BHS
1. 76.11	76.12

Eloah

	RSV	BHS

Elohenu (our God)

	1. 18.31	18.32

RSV	BHS		2. 50.22	—
1. 18.31	18.32	3. 114.7	—
2. 20.05	20.06	4. 139.19	—

Psalms Index

Authors Index